Gay Theology Without Apology

Gay Theology
Without Apology

Gary David Comstock

THE PILGRIM PRESS
CLEVELAND, OHIO

The Pilgrim Press, Cleveland, Ohio 44115
© 1993 by Gary David Comstock

Printed in the United States of America
The paper used in this publication is acid free and meets the minimum
requirements of American National Standard for Information
Sciences-Permanence of Paper for Printed Library Materials, ANSI
Z39.48-1984

98 97 96 95 94 93   5 4 3 2 1

Library of Congress Cataloging-in-Publication Data

Comstock, Gary David, 1945–
    Gay theology without apology / Gary David Comstock.
      p.   cm.
    Includes bibliographical references and index.
    ISBN 0-8298-0944-9 (alk. paper)
    1. Homosexuality—Religious aspects—Christianity.   2. Gays—
Religious life.   I. Title.
BR115.H6C673   1993
230'.08'664—dc20   92-42621
                                                                CIP

For and because of Ted

Contents

Introduction

In 1983, DURING THE EARLY STAGES of the AIDS epidemic, I was a volunteer counselor for the Gay Men's Health Crisis (GMHC) in New York City. For over a year, I visited, talked with, encouraged, ran errands for, and consoled Estaban, a very poor Puerto Rican gay man who lived in a single-room occupancy (SRO) hotel and waited for his lover to get out of prison. Estaban died before his lover returned, but not without surviving several hospital stays and moves to different hotels. Each hospitalization brought a similar cycle of descending consequences. Finding a hospital to admit him was difficult because few of them wanted or knew how to respond to AIDS and because he had no money or health insurance. During each hospital stay, Estaban would lose his hotel room and whatever public assistance he had been receiving. So that he could leave the hospital, a social worker would find him a new room in another hotel; each was worse than the one he had lived in before.

Going again through the process of applying for assistance exhausted him. He simply did not have the physical strength to take public transportation, to go to appointments, and to sit in waiting rooms. Food stamps and rent money came sporadically and only after long delays. With an immune system that was rapidly deteriorating and unable to resist a series of infectious diseases, Estaban survived in filthy, unsafe, noisy hotels whose communal bathrooms and kitchens were unusable. He was afraid to go out because his appearance bore the marks of his diseases; once he was attacked and robbed of his food stamps on the way to buy food. He lived under the pressure of continual demands for rent money; of not having enough food; of physical weakness, discomfort, and pain; and of fearing he would not see or talk to his lover again.

But Estaban did not take on the role of victim. He would get angry, but he would not whine. He did not defer to the authority of the many professionals—doctors, nurses, social workers—with whom he had to interact. He kidded his doctors, gossiped with his nurses, and had me deal with his social worker. He did not let them or me think we were doing him a favor, that we were doing unusual or good deeds, or that we were helping the unfortunate. Estaban deflated any higher ground that we might have assumed and rendered our relationships with him familiar by his own preferred manner and topics of discussion. Whether they wanted to or not, his doctors inevitably became involved in talking about what they were wearing, how they looked, and how their love life was going; and they ended up enjoying these conversations! Estaban made sure that he would be dispensing his own advice if he was going to have to be taking theirs from them. He would give as much as he took. And the doctors and nurses liked and respected him. They admired his strength to be his own person. In his own words, Estaban was a "proud and outrageous queen." I do not think it ever occurred to him that he should give up his identity to fit into other people's expectations of him. He never apologized for who he was.

Estaban defined our relationship. He needed someone to talk to on a regular basis, someone with whom he could "dish the dirt" and feel comfortable. Our "counseling sessions" were quite simply the kind of conversations that I shared with many other gay men—about our childhood, coming-out experiences, past boyfriends, how we were feeling. But in the absence of his lover and because his friends had become scarce, our getting together on a regular basis to relax and talk about what was familiar to both of us was important. Just how important became evident when I was out of town a few times and substitute counselors temporarily replaced me. None of them lasted; Estaban, I was informed, would not cooperate and told them not to come back. I do not think that Estaban preferred me because I was a better counselor, but because I did not try to change him. I did not give him advice, did not try to be his therapist, did not judge, and did not think I had a better way for doing things than what he was doing. The counseling approach and suggestions that we learned in our GMHC training workshops about building hope and developing a regular daily schedule seemed inappropriate for the overwhelming conditions under which Estaban was living. What Estaban needed and what I provided was company. I simply dropped by on a regular basis—preferably with a milk shake and hamburger— to chat, gossip, be there. I was a steady, undemanding friend.

We did disagree on one point. I thought he would be better off in the hospital on a long-term basis. It was cleaner, and he was fed and cared for there. He protested my efforts to get him into the hospital; and those times when he had to go in because of a new infection, he would quickly make arrangements to get out, even though it meant entering again into the uncertainty of a different hotel and loss of assistance. After several go-rounds with Estaban about this, I finally realized that I looked at SRO hotels as a temporary stop, something that people worked their way out of. For Estaban SRO hotels had been home for him and his lover for ten years. Estaban was not thinking of a better place to live, he was trying to maintain or get back to what he called home. In the hospital he felt as though as he did not have control; he said someone was always telling him what and when to eat, sticking him with needles, or taking a sample for another test. The SRO hotel was a familiar setting in which he made his own decisions. But most important to him—more important than getting good care and regular meals in a hospital—was to have a place ready for him and his lover when his lover got out of jail.

Although I knew that Estaban was not going to live to see his lover again, I could also see that having and keeping a place ready for them to live in was the most important project in his life. It was what he lived for. And so, I did what I could to be with him and to help him do that. When Estaban died, I tried to let his lover know. Because neither Estaban nor I were his blood relatives, and because I was not on his lover's approved list of correspondents, I was never able to get word to him.

My relationship with Estaban took place in my first year of doctoral studies at Union Theological Seminary. The following chapters were written several years later, after I had received my degree. But Estaban is the model for the unapologetic approach that I take. The "gay theology without apology" that I develop here examines the Bible and Christianity not with the purpose of fitting in or finding a place in them, but of fitting them into and changing them according to the particular experiences of lesbian/bisexual/gay people.

Christian Scripture and tradition are not authorities from which I seek approval; rather, they are resources from which I seek guidance and learn lessons as well institutions that I seek to interpret, shape, and change. I am not afraid to look for, face, and criticize those parts of Scripture and tradition that condemn us or treat us badly. I also think it is necessary to look deeply into Scripture and into our past for those affirming words that have been obscured by traditional interpretations. I initiate and develop this discussion on what may be called my own terms, that is, from the point of view of my own experience, interests, needs, and biases. These may not—and probably are not—the same as others', and I do not mean to suggest that others should take on or wear my findings; but I do want to encourage others to approach and develop theology from their own experience, interests, needs, and concerns. I do not think we need to agree theologically, but we do need to listen to each others' theologies.

I find theologian Paul Tillich helpful when he says that one's "ultimate concern" is one's God.[1] The seriousness and importance of our concerns are what require us to approach Scripture and tradition on our terms. To do otherwise is to flatten and misrepresent ourselves. Even if I could have convinced Estaban to accept and do what I thought he should do, it would have robbed him of what was most important in his life and stopped him from doing what he needed to do. We do not need to give each other the correct theological understanding; rather, we need to encourage each other to understand what is most important to us and to develop our lives around it.

The following chapters put forth *a* particular gay theology—an understanding of my ultimate concern—and make no claim to be *the* definitive gay theology. My intention is not to speak for others, but to add my voice to others' and to encourage others to speak. The comments I do make about collective lesbian/gay experience are my personal view, and I do not claim universal accuracy for them. I wrote these chapters within a five-year period at the end of the 1980s and the beginning of the 1990s, a personally secure and professionally productive time for me. I was finding firm ground on which to stand as an openly gay man; I had been ordained and was employed as a college chaplain and professor. These accomplishments were not gained without problems, obstacles, rejections, setbacks, and worry, but enough people helped at key times to produce positive outcomes.

When I worked for GMHC I met another volunteer who became my lover. Without his steadiness and support, I would have lost my bearings and courage during the ecclesiastical councils, interviews, research, writing, and manuscript submissions. Although I was sure that I wanted to become ordained as an openly gay man and work as an openly gay scholar, the doubts, misgivings, and discouragement along the way were numerous. It is ironic, perhaps, that the one who steadied and walked me safely along this bumpy road of Christian and academic institutions is Jewish; but it is also ultimately gratifying and meaningful. To survive and flourish, the relationships of gay men often transcend or dismiss the rigidity and insularity of established categories—including those of organized religion. Loyalty to affection, rather than to sectarian and denominational characteristics, counters the separation and division bred by these categories.

Such loyalty, affection, and relationship have helped me to identify my ultimate concern, to understand what is necessary and important for me to live as a full human being, to relate and be responsible to others. To be accepted, supported, and producing/ contributing are what define me as most fully human and lend ultimate meaning to my life. And it is the interface of all three— acceptance, support, and productivity—not one or the other, that is necessary for wholeness. To be accepted as a gay man without the support and means to produce and contribute means little; to produce and contribute without being able to identify as gay robs my work of an important dimension. Furthermore, to be accepted, supported and engaged in productive work allows and encourages me to accept, support, and receive the work of others—to understand that Estaban's successful efforts to keep a home ready for him and his lover are not less or more important than my research, ordination, or job. The formation of relationships and the building of community that both result in and provide for acceptance, support, and productivity are the central themes developed and discussed in the following chapters.

"Exodus and Resurrection: Transforming Pain and Suffering" identifies the primary biblical events and ethical norm by which Christians live and suggests a relationship with Scripture that is modeled on friendship rather than parental authority. "Acknowledging Biblical Bias: Constructing a Christian Sexual Ethics" addresses those biblical passages that are dangerous for lesbian/gay/ bisexual people and identifies a biblical basis for giving and receiving body pleasure. "'And Vashti Refused': Rewriting the Stories of the Silenced" finds a role model for lesbians and gay men and reclaims and retells Vashti's story in our own. "Lessons from Leviticus: Learning about the Misuse of Power" looks at the circumstances under which the most explicit antigay biblical prohibitions were written and suggests some parallels with and warnings for our own times.

"Seeing through the Camouflage: Jonathan as Unconventional Nurturer" identifies the possible outline of a fellow lover and inspiration for gay men today. "Leaving Jesus: A Theology of Friendship and Autonomy" replaces adoration and obedience with responsibility for loving others in our understanding and remembrance of Jesus. "Salvation: Embodying Our Deepest Knowledge" attempts to discuss Scripture, tradition, and salvation in non-Christian terms but with a Christian point of departure. The concluding "Credo: The Creative and Saving Spirit of Community" relies on traditional Christian terms of trinity, sin, salvation, grace, crucifixion, resurrection, and the sacraments to discuss mutuality and reciprocity in our relationships and communities.

1

Exodus and Resurrection: Transforming Pain and Suffering

LISTENING AND RELATING TO STORIES

OUR LIVES AS CHRISTIANS are born of two events: one is the exodus of slaves out of Egypt into the struggle of the wilderness and the freedom of the promised land; the other is the ministry, crucifixion, and resurrection of Jesus. For us these events are historically certain, as well as recurring and immediate. They anchor us in a past as well as shape our lives. They are the ethical norms by which we live as Christians.

Christian ethicist James Nelson defines norms as criteria or standards of judgment "which can be . . . thought about, talked about, and used . . . in decision making." Norms usually take the form of principles or rules. A principle is general and "does not specify particular actions," but rather "asserts certain moral qualities," such as kindness and respect, that should be applied to a range of activities and situations. A rule, on the other hand, is "action-specific" and "names certain . . . actions . . . as obligatory or permissible or forbidden."[1]

As ethical norms the Exodus and Jesus events function as a principle. To be sure, each of these events as told in the Bible is a compilation of stories within which one can find a variety of principles and rules; but common and central to each of these events is the unacceptability of pain and suffering inflicted upon one person or people by another. Pain or suffering is the human experience upon which these events turn; and each turns to alter it.

Without the oppression of slavery the story of the Exodus would be a rather straightforward travelogue of a people's moving from one place to another. Even as a journey with considerable hardships and special circumstances, it would not merit the significance it has for us unless it was first and foremost a story of liberation and change from slavery to freedom. Likewise, if the story of Jesus were simply a story about a man who welcomed and healed the outcast, but was not murdered, or simply a story about a man who was killed, and not because he rescued, helped, and healed others, it would not have the power to affect us. Without all three parts—his ministry to broken, neglected people; the violent opposition to that ministry; and the continuation of that ministry after his death—the story would not have the power to define who we are.

Both the Exodus and the life, death, and resurrection of Jesus are events or stories about overcoming and transforming pain, suffering, and death. Christians as people who are born of these events, therefore, are not those who bear or endure pain; they are those who transform it.

Certainly, we could not imagine the Old or New Testament without either of these respective events. Yahweh's frequent admonition and reminder to welcome the stranger because we were once strangers ourselves in the land of Egypt,[2] and Paul's persistent preaching of Christ crucified and risen,[3] underscore that which is at the heart of the Bible.

There is, of course, an abundance of other biblical material that does not bear directly on these two events. Some of it comforts, supports, and soothes us; and we are prone to lift up those parts. Some of it causes discomfort; and we are prone to ignore or trivialize those parts. Perhaps like me, you regard the liberative passages with more favor than the oppressive and have justified dismissing the less desirable as irrelevant, out of date, or vague.

But I suspect that I have been motivated by other than what can honestly be called interest in an accurate reading. As part of a lingering desire to regard the Bible as a parental authority from which I wanted and needed approval and permission, I have tended to compromise it and myself. I have been more willing to apologize for it than to criticize it; and I have been slow to admit or accept the Bible's bias against homosexuality. I have, in turn, come to terms with that bias by consciously changing my relationship with the Bible—and that change has meant a more intimate reading of and relationship with it.

Instead of making the Bible into a parental authority, I have begun to engage it as I would a friend—as one to whom I have made a commitment and in whom I have invested dearly, but with whom I insist on a mutual exchange of critique, encouragement, support, and challenge. Such investment and commitment hinge on deeply felt and shared experience, meaning, and outlook—a cooperative project to live fully that both changes and remains steady through joys and sorrow. The connection I have shared with some friends and family members has been so vital and meaningful that troubled times, disagreements, and shortcomings have been tolerated, invited, and worked through precisely so that the relationship would not only endure, but continue to grow, change, and become richer. Some of those disagreements have been over homophobia. It has been important for me not to let my friends and family members get away with attitudes, thinking, and behaviors that oppress and diminish lesbians and gay men. Perhaps James Baldwin best captures my meaning when he says, "If I love you, I have to make you conscious of the things you do not see."[4] I worked through those problems because I valued my relationship with these people and because their homophobia was a contradiction to that combination of experience, meaning, outlook, and project that we otherwise shared.

The Exodus and Jesus events represent a similar combination of experience, meaning, outlook, and project that I share, commit to, invest in, and because of which I grow, change, and struggle. As with my friends, I cannot take the relationship lightly, nor will I give it up quickly; and as with my friends, I criticize and call it to account for its homophobia. Although its homophobic statements sting and condemn me, I counter that those statements are themselves condemned by its own Exodus and Jesus events. Just as I have said to my friends, "How can you express love and be a justice-seeking person and not work to overcome the oppression of lesbian and gay men?" in my dialogue with the Bible I ask, "How can you be based on two events that are about transforming pain, suffering, and death into life, liberation, and healing, and yet call for the misery and death of lesbians and gay men?"

Two stories told to me during my childhood by my mother illustrate the kind of relationship with the Bible I am proposing. Both are about events that occurred in a small New England town in the 1920s and 30s. The first had to do with my mother's experience as a girl being raised by her mother in a community in which people knew she had been conceived out of wedlock. I remember being told of one incident in which she was teased about this by a friend on the playground at school. I find it significant that my mother told this story at all, for I would not have heard about it on my own and then gone to her for an explanation. It was, therefore, her purposely selected lesson for me in values, survival, and growth beyond social disapproval. In the telling of the story my mother never placed any blame on her mother, nor did she feel any shame herself. The story instead turned on two other points—one, that those who disapproved were wrong; and two, that my mother never gave in to the disapproval, but rather rose above it to become a respected community leader herself. The lesson or message of the other story she told was similar, but from her high school days. It was about her speech for an oratorical contest that was titled "If I were in love with a Negro, would I marry him?" Her conclusion was, "Yes, of course." Her telling of this story turned not on the content of the speech, but on the reaction to it. Her emphasis fell on the shock and criticism of teachers and students, which made her stand by her position even more strongly.

These stories have been powerful influences in my life, and their bearing on my coming out as a gay man should be obvious. But my purpose in citing them is to show that my mother established some very definite norms with these stories with which I would interpret and shape the world I inherited and with which I would respond to other people and situations. With these stories or norms she also effectively defined herself and what I could expect from her.

On the other hand, my mother and father were as homophobic as the next person and certainly raised me with a clearly stated heterosexist agenda. But her stories were more normative and lasting for me than the cultural conformity to post-World-War-II hetero-sexuality in which I grew up. The stories were special, told and retold in a manner that gave them lasting meaning. And because they established a norm and center of who she was, I would later not only be able, but feel compelled, to challenge her to live according to them and change her own homophobia—which she has done; in fact, it was she, not I, who first broached the subject of my gayness after a number of my visits home from San Francisco. And so, we have changed each other—she to accept and integrate a gay son into the family structure; and I not to be afraid to share myself and talk openly with relatives.

I pose a similar challenge in a similar way and for similar reasons to the Bible. As a patriarchal document that places great value on men heading families and women bearing children, the Bible's ho-mophobia should not surprise me, any more than I should be surprised that my parents subscribed to the post-World-War-II nuclear-family, child-rearing cultural model and raised me as a heterosexual son. Parts of my upbringing may make me angry, but they should not surprise me; they should make me want to make changes. I counter and criticize the Bible's bias in terms of the stories of the Exodus and Jesus events, just as I criticized my mother's homophobia in terms of her stories. Not to criticize the bias, either by acceding to it or by simply dismissing and ignoring it, is to turn our backs on the tools or norms with which we can transform pain and suffering into life, healing, and liberation. These stories are what compel us to examine and to say that we reject such prescriptions as "If a man lies with a male as with a woman, both of them have committed an abomination; they shall be put to death, their blood is upon them" (Lev. 20:13),[5] because they engender wrong, painful, static suffering.

Christian ethicist Beverly Harrison reminds us that norms or principles can be used either "for the purpose of terminating the process of moral reasoning . . . to invoke the principle [that] settles the matter, stops debate," or, conversely, "to open up processes of reasoning rather than close them down . . . to help locate and weigh values, to illuminate a range of values that always inhere in significant human decisions." The Leviticus passage orders, closes down, ends discussion. Because the Exodus and Jesus events are made up of a variety of stories and presented from various viewpoints and because the transformation of pain and suffering is a "broad, generalized moral criteri[on]" rather than a "narrower, specific prescription,"[6] they are a resource that requires both ongoing study and clarification as well as thoughtful reconsideration for and application to our present and changing personal/social contexts.[7]

The kind of relationship with the Bible that I am suggesting cannot be made without discussion, conflict, and examination with others in community; without its own consequences of challenging, offending, and feeling at odds with others; without effort, strength, and resources that are years in the making. The relationship is not progressive and linear, but rather a recurring and often slowly building process, continually resurrected by the need for suffering and pain to be changed.

BREAKING AWAY AND COMING OUT

In 1951 when I was six years old, I was becoming aware of the first feelings of the pain and fear of being different, and I was beginning to develop those protective strategies that would allow me to forge an acceptable identity, to conceal and reshape my affections, thoughts, and dreams. As a young person growing up in a small New England town, I kept within me the fear that I would be discovered and expelled from the community. No one knew the horror that I kept hidden, but at that time on the West Coast many miles away from where I lived, a group of lesbians and gay men stood in a circle, holding hands in a candlelit room, and pledged themselves to the following:

> *Our interlocking, sustaining and protecting hands guarantee a reborn social force of immense and single purpose. We are resolved that our people shall find equality of security and production in tomorrow's world. We are sworn that no boy or girl, approaching the maelstrom of deviation, need make that crossing alone, afraid and in the dark ever again. In these moments we dedicate ourselves once again to each other in the immense significance of such allegiance, with dignity and respect, proud and free.*[8]

Unknown to me and unheard by me at the time as a six-year-old, these original members of the Mattachine Society had issued the words and laid the groundwork for the transformation of my pain that would occur twenty years later. In time I would find it necessary to leave church, family, and hometown and travel three thousand miles to begin my life as a gay man. That it would not happen until I was twenty-six speaks of having borne a pain and heeded the advice of Leviticus instead of the pain-changing power of Exodus and Jesus. It was not until I left that I began to be a Christian, if we understand Christians to be those who transform pain.

Several decisions and stops brought me there. The Vietnam War involved me in making what I saw as the first independent and most important decision of my life. While I was a graduate student at Cornell, I protested the war by returning my draft card to my draft board. No one in my family understood or approved. I was subsequently called up for and I refused induction into the army. I was tried, convicted, and sentenced to zero to six years under the Youth Correction Act.[9] I did not serve any time because the U.S. Supreme Court eventually decided that punitive reclassification and induction were unconstitutional.

I was active in poverty programs and peace projects. The last and largest national anti-Vietnam War demonstration in Washington in 1971 was to have a significant impact on me. Unlike previous marches, lesbians and gay men were prominent in the organizing and publicity leading up to this one. At the march I was arrested for civil disobedience like thousands of others. As I stood in long lines waiting to be bused to jail, and as I sat for hours in holding tanks waiting to be arraigned, I watched for the first time in my life groups of gay men shouting, laughing, chanting "Gay Power!" I was moved by gay solidarity and celebration, by gay people who were sure enough of themselves to move confidently among and for others. Although I was not sure enough of myself to interact with them there, they were an example of activism and unabashedness that I could not resist.

Soon after this I moved to Seattle where my closest friends from Cornell were now living and doing community organizing. I told them that I was planning to come out and received their support, but I was terrified of losing them and of entering another culture that was still unknown to me. Some of my friends said they could put me in touch with gay people they knew, but I continued to hang on, developing pointless crushes on my straight male friends. The final nudge came when I visited one of my friends who was in jail for antiwar work. She had a way of being concerned but impatient. "Stop stalling," she said.

I first experienced community when I finally worked up the courage to walk through the door of a gay bar in Seattle. The feeling was one of being home finally—of letting go of denial and hiding. The bar was in the sleazy part of town; it had no sign, simply a nondescript door on the side of a seemingly unused building. By stepping inside I began to become what I had always feared. With relief, and also with a measure of trembling, I was finding my own salvation—joining the company of the despised and finding sensitive, intelligent, and friendly people to love.

New friends and first lovers introduced me to my body. But it was neither an all-at-once nor a smooth transition. I could not accept myself totally after having developed and relied on camouflaging strategies for so many years. In one of my moments of copping to a straight identity and the privileges that go with it, a lover once gently reminded me, "Remember, hon, you're just a queen like the rest of us." Much time, many friends, lovers, and experiences would pass before I would be content, comfortable, at rest with myself as a gay man; before I would relax into the fullness and specialness of my ordinary self;[10] before I would remember the words at the end of the sixth day of the creation story—"And God saw everything that God had made, and behold, it was very good" (Gen. 1:31)—and know that I was a part of what is very good, that I was a good creation.

A friend and I eventually moved to San Francisco. I had this inverted American dream of finding a nice husband with a cottage and white picket fence and settling down for the rest of my life. That illusion quickly gave way to immersion in the unprecedented tribal gathering of lesbians and gay men that was happening in the formation of the Castro neighborhood. By hanging out on the streets on any given afternoon one could meet other gay men from anywhere in the country. I formed a household with five others. Two were high school runaways, a Latino from Houston and an African-American Filipino from Los Angeles. Both had survived their first months in the city by hustling. Another was a white working-class young man fresh out of high school from Vermont. The others were a forty-year-old hospital worker from Butte who had just broken up with his lover of twenty years and a former high school teacher from a Chicago suburb who had been discreetly dismissed on the basis of false allegations about sexual activity with a student. And myself, fleeing from the East Coast, inappropriately equipped with an upper-middle-class education to grow with these five people into our experience of what family really meant to us. This assortment of folks had not been assembled with an eye to "diversity," but was instead the unplanned outcome of the usual interactions of street life and nightlife in the gay ghetto at that time.

We thought of ourselves as "sisters," not because we had become women, but because the customary definition of brothers fell short of the way we shared our lives. As that which is usually considered masculine relaxed, that which is usually thought of as feminine was affirmed. Those ways of thinking, acting, feeling, and being affectionate that had not happened in our biological families happened here. We learned that each of us at early ages had learned to pretend and act our ways through childhood and high school. Although none of us were lovers or sexual partners with the others, we spoke, touched, relaxed, and shared our lives in ways and more deeply than we had ever done before. There was no need to guard speech, to keep secrets, to be cautious or ashamed. We also ventured to be silly and marvelous. One night as we got ready to go to a party, Patrick made available his collection of ball gowns. With excitement and nervousness we all went in dresses—not to mock or imitate women but to stop mocking ourselves, to stop worshiping the trappings and security of divisions that precisely define maleness and femaleness. We came alive; we were animated; we had so much fun that the demons fled. We slew the dragon that restricts adornment.

The subsequent years of building new relationships and interests were a formative time of healing and nurture for me. Immersed in the gay community of San Francisco, to go about one's daily business and not have to encounter straight people was an undreamed of relief from a past of having twisted myself every which way to fit in. In time, buoyed, healed, and strengthened, I journeyed back to church, home, and family of origin.

Both in terms of my personal growth and in terms of the growth of the lesbian/gay community itself, a dissatisfaction with our conditional freedom to love whom we wanted in isolated pockets of urban culture here and there would propel us into the public realm of social institutions, including the church. There was among us a brewing sense that we wanted to be gay and lesbian not only to each other, but in the world—a part of a wider community, not just accepted by it, but contributing to it and shaping it. As we moved back and out to reclaim full community status, we were not simply returning, but returning as new people and with the purpose not simply of fitting into old institutions but of changing them, so that they no longer would be places in which children grew up hating and distorting themselves, bearing their pain silently. And we began to return not only so that lesbians and gay men would be able to live in community with others, but so that others would be able to live in community with us, so that the lives of others would be fuller having us in their midst. The thrust of this new impulse in the movement was born of our experience as lesbians and gay men together, in which we had demonstrated to each other that we were creative, capable people.

We moved, therefore, with the belief that we have a valuable contribution to make to others and that others have a responsibility to make a contribution to our lives. In theological and biblical terms, it is said no better than by Paul himself:

For in one body we have many members, and all the members do not have the same function, so we, though many, are one body in Christ [or in community], and individually members one of another. Being favored with different gifts, let us use them. (Rom. 12:4-6a)[11]

The church or any community is a dead and nonresurrected body without us. For lesbians and gay men to return to and live within the church without declaring, celebrating, and sharing their affectional identities would make as little sense as reading and remembering the Exodus story and omitting any references to slavery. Our being openly lesbian and gay is important not only because it helps us and others to understand who we are, but also why we are here, and what in our experience is vital and valuable for the church to know in its mission of transforming pain and suffering. In some ways lesbians and gay men know what no others know, just as others know what we do not but need to know. Without us the church is partial. Together we can get on with the business of building community and making justice and peace.

COMING BACK AND BUILDING COMMUNITY

On my way to seminary fourteen years ago I picked up a copy of Henry Nouwen's *Creative Ministry*. As I was reading it the summer before my first semester, one passage summarized for me what I had learned coming out as a gay man and what would be central to my understanding and practice of ministry. Nouwen cites the familiar passage from Acts 20:35 in which Jesus is reported to have said, "It is more blessed to give than to receive," and then, in a twist of conventional interpretation and flash of common sense, Nouwen says:

> It is difficult to recognize the meaning of Jesus' saying . . . because it is difficult to confess that perhaps the greatest service we can offer to [people] is to receive and allow them the happiness of giving. For much of the happiness in our lives is derived from the fact that we can give and that our friends are willing to receive our gifts, to make them a part of their lives, and to allow themselves to become dependent on us through them. . . . A gift only becomes a gift when it is received; and nothing we have to give . . . will ever be recognized as true gifts until someone opens [his or her] hands and heart to accept them. This all suggests that [the one] who wants someone else to grow—that is, to discover [her or] his potential and capacities, to experience that [she or] he has something to live and work for— should first of all be able to recognize that person's gifts and be willing to receive them. For [a person] only becomes fully [human] when [she or] he is received and accepted.[12]

If there is a single Christian duty, task, or project, it is not to give to others, but to create and be in community in which people can give, contribute, and feel valuable. I understand Christian ministry to be the building of community in which people are encouraged to participate and contribute, to share and develop themselves, to be taken seriously, to take others seriously, to recognize and be recognized. In using Paul's metaphor of the body of Christ for community, this ministry would be considered resurrectional ministry— that is, the continual making, expanding, and enriching of community, the raising up of community through the ongoing task of including and empowering its members. In Exodus terms, it would be a ministry of moving out of the bondage, alienation, and separation into the freedom of whole community, into the freedom of being who we are and can be, with and because of others.

This is not a one-way ministry, either from the affluent to the needy, from the experts to the ill informed, from the top to the bottom, or from the bottom to the top; it is instead ministry among people, an interactive ministry in which each life has the potential to impact and change another. It is not a ministry to people, but a ministry by, with, and among people. A ministry that is conceived as being to any particular group of people creates and sustains these people as victims; it sees needs as requiring correction rather than as resources for changing others, changing structures. Ministry by, or at least with, people acknowledges that they have something to teach or give—some suggestion, insight, plan, experience, or knowledge that can change us, change the church, transform pain and suffering.

With Jesus who brings our attention to the most unlikely inheritors of God's realm—

> *The disciples rebuked the people who brought children to him, but he said, "Let the children come to me, for to such belongs the realm of heaven." (Mark 10:13)[13]*

—and with Isaiah who foresaw that a little child would lead us into the peaceful community—

> *The wolf shall dwell with the lamb, and the leopard shall lie down with the kid, and the calf and the lion and the fatling together, and a little child shall lead them. (Isa. 11:6)[14]*

—and with Latin American liberation theologians who recognize the epistemological advantage of the oppressed to know what is wrong and how to transform injustice,[15] I understand ministry as recognizing and facilitating the power of the disempowered to change our lives, and joining with them in the project of making changes that will change us both.

That which is central to my personal journey, to my understanding of ministry, and to my call to ministry can be stated in two ways: (1) as the *refusal* to be isolated—either as a frightened, hiding person in a closet or as a gay man living for the most part exclusively with other gay men in a gay ghetto; or (2) as the *insistence* to live among all people—to touch and be touched, to influence and be influenced by a community as diverse as God's creation, to recognize the notion of difference as a dynamic divine/human force, one that is enriching rather than threatening. In the words of African-American lesbian poet Audre Lorde:

> We know that human differences have been used to separate and confuse us. We have typically responded to difference either by ignoring it and going about our normal lives, or we have tried to copy it if we think it dominant, or destroyed it if we think it's subordinate.[16]

We have typically resisted and had problems with creating the patterns and building the community for relating across human differences as equals, not simply to tolerate difference, but to live as if we could not survive without those who are not like ourselves. Within an interactive, expanding ministry, a question that I often hear—"Can the church survive the lesbian/gay issue?"—has no place; and one hears, instead, the concern, "How can we ever survive or how can we live as full human beings without lesbians and gay men in the church?"

To do other than to insist on identifying as an openly gay member of the clergy would be to deny the very experience and relationships that have created me, made me who I am, and, also, to deny other people the creative experience of relating to me as a unique, fully human being with valuable gifts and vast potential. Lesbians and gay men—or anyone living in an interactive community in which we encourage and receive the gifts of others and work to eliminate the need for hiding, discretion, and fear—have to give, be open, be unafraid to reveal the source and depths of our dreams and fantasies. To live so inclusively is motivated not only by our need to be ourselves and to know others, but by the need of others to know us if they are to be themselves. Our living as open lesbians and gay men in the church is not simply a personal choice and struggle; in Christian terms, it is a communal decision that will affect, change, and create others. For lesbians and gay men not to insist on being open in the church robs or violates that community as much as do the efforts of nongay/lesbian people to keep us out.

As a seminary student pastor doing my field education work, I was counseled by my supervisor not to make my affectional orientation known to the small rural parish I was to serve. I was an openly gay man within the seminary community. But he said it would do no one in the parish any good to know about it. And I concurred. This concession made me a faceless liar, for one is never a neutral person in a neutral situation—one goes into a situation in which heterosexuality is assumed. There is no labelless utopia: if you do not name or label yourself, the world will do it for you. Without anyone specifically asking you to go along with the ubiquitous joke, remark, or invitation that are common parlance, you find yourself identified according to convention. The first query that goes something like, "When are you going to find a nice girlfriend?" and that you somewhat uncomfortably but politely let pass, within time becomes a game, with real stakes, that you find yourself eventually immersed in, hating, and fearing its next occurrence. I was tense, never felt real, and was angry for having gotten into the mess.

Those who maintain that what we do sexually is a private matter, and does not or should not make any difference to our ministry, overlook the fact that the sexuality of ministry is not neutrally perceived. The ministry that we have been brought up on was assumed to be heterosexual. Although it was never said, everyone assumed that they knew what ministers did in the privacy of their bedrooms. We have insisted that our ministers be married and preferably with children—but we have not had to be vocally insistent about that because our ministers have usually come in those packages. Protestant ministry is based on a tradition of heterosexual practice. Because Protestant denominations have traditionally assumed to know what its ministers are doing in their bedrooms, the matter was rarely, if ever, a question or point that was addressed or discussed.

I maintain that what a minister or anyone does in his or her bedroom is very important. I do not know if it has to be publicly discussed, but I do feel that a person's intimate, physical relationships should not have to be separated from her or his other experiences and relationships. I assume that the issues of sharing, cooperation, reciprocity, mutuality, control, vulnerability, and giving and receiving of pleasure that fuel and are the dynamnics of sexuality would be exactly those personal issues with which ministers and people in their communities are struggling. Why should this rich and vital human activity of God's creation be off limits? Our lovemaking, desires for and experiences of physical pleasure, and the people with whom we form primary affectional-sexual relationships greatly affect and are rich resources for our ministries. Keeping silent about those areas of human activity, we neglect an important point of dialogue with each other and a resource for building communities in which effective sharing is necessary.

I would also say, however, that being a gay minister has less to do with being sexually candid and more simply to do with being generally relaxed and open. I am not talking about wearing a placard around one's neck or focusing one's ministry on sexual issues. I mean feeling free to choose from the full range of one's experiences, sensitivities, and skills, and not always having to be self-consciously selective, guarded, or fearful of candid self-expression. I am merely talking about a ministry in which a minister lives, works, and plays fully as her or himself—as a whole, and not partial person, for whom her or his affections, fantasies, imagination, and dreams are an active resource inspiring and shaping ministry—as a person who draws from her or his own experience instead of from that which is fabricated, expected, or assumed.

But I do not think that the resistance to ordaining lesbians and gay men as ministers—to accepting us as fully involved leaders and facilitators of community in the church—is motivated by concerns about sexual propriety, free expression, and affectional permissiveness, as much as it is by a concern that the current arrangement of power within denominations will be threatened and undermined. As people who simply want either to have sex with each other or to establish our own affectional bonds, lesbians and gay men can perhaps in time be tolerated; but as people who want to be part of the community with decision-making power and influence, we are talking about a more substantial challenge to the established order. When gay men and lesbians are asking for permission from the church for a sexual/affectional life-style, we are dealing with issues of tolerance and acceptance. However, when we give ourselves permission for our sexual and affectional behavior and press not for acceptance but for equal decision-making and leadership status in the church, then we have an issue that shakes the church to its foundations. Then we learn that being heterosexually identified is an important, if not necessary, condition for power and influence.

Heterosexuality, as a credential for leadership and ministry within the church, is so taken for granted that it is not even thought of or discussed until lesbians and gay men apply for such positions. It then becomes crystal clear that heterosexual orientation is indeed a necessary qualification for leadership and power. If this were not true, why would most lesbians and gay men conceal their sexual/affectional orientation so that they can move into the ordained ministry and other church jobs? The tenacity with which closeted lesbians and gay men in the church cling to their closets testifies to the fact that to have power, to be a leader, or to be employed in the church requires heterosexual identification, or at the least no overt homosexual identification. Whether one is pretending to be heterosexual or actually is, both stand to gain position and privilege because of it.

My understanding and learning of the need for lesbians and gay men to be "out" as ministers, however, did not come from an analysis of denominational structures and power arrangements. It came from my experience as a closeted student pastor, from the fear that there would be gay men and lesbians in the parish who specifically needed contact and counseling with me as a gay man and that I would not be an identifiable resource for them nor free to reach out to them. I was deeply bothered that I was not being the kind of minister who would have made all the difference in the world to me as a child growing up in a small town. I had been starved for adults who, by living openly as gay men and lesbians, would have transformed my world of pain. And there I was, in my student parish, sustaining the world of pain and silence. The experience presented the opportunity to decide again for Exodus and resurrection, to transform pain and suffering, to change and rebuild community, to lift up and take seriously the gifts of all members of the community. To be out at all times within the church, to risk being denied ordination and employment, to engage in the fight for basic rights and participation for lesbians and gay men within the church—these were to be integral parts of the ministry to which I had been called by the pain and suffering of my people and the liberation movement that had begun to transform it.

2

Acknowledging Biblical Bias: Constructing a Christian Sexual Ethics

GIVING AND RECEIVING BODY PLEASURE

SEXUAL ETHICS IS DOING what is good, right, pleasurable with our bodies. In the exchange of and response to "yes-and-no" as we touch ourselves and others, we learn what is good and pleasurable; we construct a sexual ethics of giving and receiving body pleasure.

A social order that does not allow or encourage people to discover, experience, and enjoy their bodies deprives them of living as full human beings. [1] We live within such a social order. The sexual ethics of the social order within which we live and the sexual ethics of body pleasure are constructed quite differently—one is a set of behaviors enforced by those who control and manage the social order; the other emerges out of people's enjoyment of themselves and their interaction with and response to each other.

Not only are these two sexual ethics constructed differently, each rests upon a different value. The sexual ethics that I favor finds its meaning in our interest in our bodies and our need for body pleasure; it values all parts of the body as sources of pleasure. The sexual ethics that I oppose finds its meaning in procreation; and the genitals have exclusive or primary importance.

It is as an outsider—as an outlaw in the twenty-four states in which consensual same-sex relations are still a crime[2]—that I have come to know and value my body's goodness, its need to give and receive pleasure. During the past twenty-five years, lesbian/gay/bisexual people have embarked on a "journey without maps"[3] through forbidden and unknown land to make and claim what was not yet—to make love, to enjoy and celebrate our bodies without shame, fear, or guilt. From finding one another discretely and secretly, many of us have moved to being supported openly by one another, by a few friends, and by an emerging movement and community. Guided by our desire for physical touch, by our need for affection and company, by the few words passed on to us by those who managed to survive and affirm themselves in the decades and centuries before us,[4] and by the courageous and outrageous example and resistance of our most bold,[5] we continue to find others, to form relationships, to build the community that we had not been taught or allowed to make.[6] But the reported increase of antigay/lesbian violence nationwide, recurring campaigns to repeal and prevent passage of lesbian/gay rights legislation, the disproportionately high rate of suicide among lesbian/gay youth, and the fact that they still survive their high school years "by arming themselves with evasions and silence" are evidence that we have not yet been able to chart a safe course for ourselves.[7]

If our experience as outsiders is the source of knowledge from which we see and build alternatives to procreative, genitally focused heterosexuality, our view is not without recognition and support from established sources. Freud, for example, found that the interests and histories of many of his clients ran counter to "the prevailing view" that same-sex relations were scarce and abhorrent, that genital orgasm was more important than touching and caressing other parts of the body, that procreation was the felt intent or purpose of sexual activity, or that children did not have sexual feelings and were not sexually active.[8] On the basis of what he saw as the socially

"neglected facts" of his research, Freud offered the following "prin-
cipal findings," which "contradicted all the popular opinions on
sexuality":

1. Sexual life does not begin at puberty but starts with plain
   manifestations soon after birth.
2. It is necessary to distinguish sharply between concepts of
   "sexual" and "genital." The former is the wider concept
   and includes many activities that have nothing to do with
   the genitals.
3. Sexual life includes the function of obtaining pleasure from
   zones of the body—a function that is subsequently brought
   into the service of reproduction. The two functions often
   fail to coincide completely.[9]

Freud's attending remark that these findings "provoked astonishment and denials" when they were released in the early twentieth
century does not seem so out of date as the century draws to a close.

CHILDREN AND BODY PLEASURE

Perhaps adults want to deny most quickly the findings of Freud
and of others about children's sexuality,[10] and they are most uncomfortable with a sexual ethics of giving and receiving body pleasure
when children are considered.[11] Maybe we too quickly imagine a
worst case scenario of adults coercing children to have genital sex
and do not consider the possibility of mutuality within the full range
of physical touch.

To be sure, this is a difficult and complex topic, and the current
increased reporting of sexual abuse of children signals the need for
caution and protective measures;[12] but the prevalence of such abuse
condemns the dominant social ethic rather than the one I am
advocating, especially since the reported abuse is predominantly the
genital penetration of girls by men.[13] Ironically, a society that
refuses to recognize the sexual feelings and needs of children appears
to be plagued by the gross violation of them. As adults we should

reconsider our reluctance and refusal to face squarely the fact that children do become genitally aroused and do enjoy body contact.

Perhaps we need to look at other cultures in which children's sexuality is permitted and integrated into the life of the community.[14] Instead of practicing flat restriction and complacent ignorance, we need to take on the more complicated task of facilitating and protecting privacy, autonomy, mutuality, and reciprocity, of permitting expression and restricting imposition. The following verses from "The Bath" by Gary Snyder may help to provide a window through which we can glimpse the positive integration of touch, body, pleasure, and negotiation in our relationships with children:

> *Washing Kai in the sauna,*
> *The kerosene lantern set on a box*
> *   outside the ground-level window,*
> *Lights up the edge of the iron stove and the*
> *   washtub down on the slab*
> *Steaming air and crackle of waterdrops*
> *   brushed by on the pile of rocks on top*
> *He stands in warm water*
> *Soap all over the smooth of his thigh and stomach*
> *   "Gary don't soap my hair!"*
> *   —his eye-sting fear—*
> *   the soapy hand feeling*
> *   through and around the globes and curves of his body*
> *   up in the crotch,*
> *And washing-tickling out the scrotum, little anus,*
> *   his penis curving up and getting hard*
> *   as I pull back skin and try to wash it*
> *Laughing and jumping, flinging arms around,*
> *   I squat all naked too,*
> >   is this our body?
>
> *Sweating and panting in the stove-steam hot-stone*
> *   cedar-planking wooden bucket water-splashing*
> *   kerosene lantern-flicker wind-in-the-pines-out*
> *   sierra forest ridges night—*

Masa comes in, letting fresh cool air
  sweep down from the door
  a deep sweet breath
And she tips him over gripping neatly, one knee down
  her hair falling hiding one whole side of
  shoulder, breast, and belly,
Washes deftly Kai's head-hair
  and he gets mad and yells—

. . . .

As Kai laughs at his mother's breast he is now weaned
  from, we
  wash each other,
                    this is our body

. . . .

Clean, and rinsed, and sweating more, we stretch
  out on the redwood benches hearts all beating
Quiet to the simmer of the stove,
  the scent of cedar
And then turn over,
  murmuring gossip of the grasses,
  talking firewood

. . . .

The cloud across the sky. The windy pines.
  the trickle gurgle in the swampy meadow

                    this is our body.

Fire inside and boiling water on the stove
We sigh and slide ourselves down from the benches
  wrap the babies, step outside,

black night & all stars.

Pour cold water on the back and thighs
Go in the house—stand steaming by the center fire
Kai scampers on the sheepskin
Gen standing hanging on and shouting,

"Bao! bao! bao! bao! bao!"

This is our body. Drawn up crosslegged by the flames
    drinking icy water
    hugging babies, kissing bellies,

Laughing on the Great Earth

Come out from the bath.[15]

I would also offer my own practical suggestion for changing the quality of touching between adults and children and for giving children power to control and modify it.

When I was a doctoral student I also taught in Union Theological Seminary's day-care center. The staff of female, male, African-American, Hispanic, white, Jewish, Christian, lesbian, gay, straight, old, and young adults attempted to create a nonsexist, multicultural curriculum built more from the children's needs and interests than from our own agenda of what we thought they should be doing and learning. We asked a team of early-childhood education experts to come in and observe our interactions with the children. Not only did they help us to see that our interactions with girls and boys differed (we were physically rougher and spent more time with the boys), but that we often touched, held, hugged, or physically directed the children without their permission. As harmless and affectionate as these casual contacts may have seemed (the typical interactions that a teacher has with children when building with blocks, reading stories, going on walks, or playing in the sandbox), we most often initiated them, and we assumed that they were good. Who would question the goodness of giving a hug, helping fill a pail with sand, or giving a child a push on a tricycle?

After discussing the power and potential misuse of it that we had simply because of our size, age, and position, the staff decided to use more and different language with the children. Instead of simply picking up, hugging, or dressing a child, we would say, "May I have a hug?" or "Will you hold my hand while we walk along the street?" or "May I button up your jacket for you?" We would look for and respect the indifference, acceptance, or resistance they felt at the time and encourage and help them to express objection, refusal, reception, appreciation. We, as teachers and as adults, realized also that we had to be candid about and explain our own wishes to be left alone or to be close, to express appreciation, disapproval, and need without rejecting, punishing, or manipulating. I offer this example as a way for us to normalize the saying and hearing of yes and no, so that children will be able to develop and use these words as a basis and resource for physical interactions and for forming sexual and affectional relations as adolescents and adults. [16]

In addition to specific suggestions such as these for daily practice, we must understand the larger sexual ethics, of which the aversion to children's sexuality is a part. The cultural and social requirement that sexual life begin after puberty, along with compulsory, genitally focused heterosexuality, defines and enforces sex as procreative. And modern Christianity has traditionally led and/or aided in enforcing it. Why is procreation the basis of sexual ethics in dominant Christian theology? [17]

THE BIBLE AS A PATRIARCHAL DOCUMENT

Historian Peter Brown has suggested that sexual renunciation, rather than procreation, was more prominent and formative in early Christian thought and communities. [18] But with the ascendance of Christianity and the demise of the Roman Empire, "a growing emphasis on procreative commitment" developed alongside of asceticism. [19] For example, "the extreme asceticism" of Augustine, the fourth-century church father, condemned as lustful "every sexual act not undertaken with procreative intent" and insisted that procreation "was the only truly moral use of sexuality."[20] His theology "set the stage for many centuries of Christian thinking."[21]

By the end of the thirteenth century, the church had gained legal jurisdiction over marriage and had appropriated Thomas Aquinas's theology of nature to regulate it. Aquinas equated "natural" with procreative sex and provided what was to be an enduring "three-fold standard for the moral judgment of sexual acts: they must be done for the right purpose (procreation), with the right person (one's lawfully-wedded spouse), and in the right way (heterosexual genital intercourse)."[22]

Subsequent to the Reformation of the sixteenth century, Protestant theologians disavowed celibacy and "endorsed the belief that divine blessing was expressed directly through progeny." The emergence of the "modern child-centered family" under late eighteenth- and nineteenth-century industrialism would lead many Christian theologians to conclude that "procreation within the context of marriage as a 'covenant' or 'sacrament' is the primal metaphor for divine blessing of human life."[23]

These theologies are often justified by reading the biblical stories through the lenses of the modern institutions of marriage and family relations, even though children in ancient patriarchal societies served the purposes of male wealth and family survival and were not seen as proof or evidence of the love, affection, and caring that "we are presumed to experience chiefly in the privatized interpersonal family sphere."[24] But though one must also overlook the practices of polygamy and concubinage in Hebrew Scripture and Paul's indifference to and warnings against marriage in the New Testament, one can easily mine the major themes and stories of the Bible to find support and a basis for today's procreative sexual ethics and male-headed nuclear family.

The Bible is, after all, a patriarchal document. The social structure of biblical times was patriarchal—a man ruled a nation as a man ruled a tribe as a man ruled his family. That the theological document to emerge from these times would be an expression by those men about their God is illustrated in the so-called "household codes" of the New Testament. In these codes wives are told to "be subject to your husbands, as is fitting in the Lord . . . for the husband is the head of the wife as Christ is the head of the church."[25] The Bible reflects the religious concerns and sociopolitical position of men; it was largely written by and addressed to them. The Bible is a product of those who controlled and managed the social order of that time.[26]

As biblical scholar Norman Gottwald observes, the prominence of women in some stories sustains rather than undermines the notion that men controlled home and society; for although "very strong women" are "as sharply etched characters as are the men," they "are forceful actors in the domestic sphere," with "significant parts to play" in and because of the affairs of men. Within Genesis, for example, the compelling acts of women—Sarah's jealousy and motherhood, Rebekah's going to Canaan to be Isaac's wife and her subsequent outsmarting of him, and Rachel and Leah's rivalry for Jacob[27]—hinge on the needs, demands, and responses of men. And even in the story of Ruth and Naomi, which is noteworthy "because these women do not wait passively for men to solve their problems," they "are able to find joyful fulfillment within the male-headed social structures in such a way that both sexes profit." Ruth's bearing a son to Boaz is "the happy coincidence of the story" that simultaneously (1) brings him the good fortune of children and prosperity, (2) provides Naomi with a grandson to care for her in her old age, and (3) consolidates a household in which she and Naomi may continue to live safely together.[28] The final lines of the Book of Ruth, however, bring into sharp focus its place and importance in the biblical canon: the son Obed is listed and has a place in the male line that leads to King David.

Biblical scholar Phyllis Trible discusses other stories in which women are prominent, but as victims of violence: "Hagar, the slave used, abused, and rejected; Tamar, the princess raped and discarded; an unnamed woman, the concubine raped, murdered, and dismembered; and the daughter of Jephthah, a virgin slain and sacrificed."[29] These "tales of terror" are not included in the Bible to serve as examples of injustice to be corrected, nor as lessons of what should not be done, but rather as incidents amid the lives of men, the consequences of being a women in a male-controlled society.

The Bible is also a humanitarian document, however, reflecting a concern for the welfare of others who are less fortunate. It consistently requires men to take care of orphans and widows, to feed the hungry and clothe the naked, to welcome the stranger.[30] Likewise, the landowner is required to let servants and animals rest for one day each week. But the humanitarianism prescribed and encouraged in the Bible maintains the power of men. Men provide for the less fortunate and less powerful. To take care of another is not the same as empowering the other to take care of her- or himself. To maintain the role of provider is to maintain power over others. The social laws are not addressed to the needy themselves and do not direct them to take control of their lives. The laws ultimately maintain the social and political position of a certain social class of men.[31]

PATRIARCHAL SEXUAL ETHICS

The protection of the social and political position of men is also strongly evidenced in the prescribed sexual behaviors in the Bible. Here, too, the rules and advice concerning sexual behavior are addressed to men. And as with the social roles, there are also humanitarian aspects to the prescribed sexual behavior. For example, prohibitions against the divorcing of women by men are often interpreted as a measure to protect women from a social environment in which they would be readily abused and neglected if left alone.[32] So, too, must the man who rapes a virgin marry her,[33] "since she is now a 'defiled' woman. Even if, by some chance, some other man were willing to marry her, she would remain highly vulnerable to being 'put away' by him when it suited him (Deut. 22:13-21)."[34] As with the socially needy, the Bible does not seek to empower women sexually; it takes care of them within a social order oriented to serving men.

In biblical sexuality the heterosexual man is central and in control. Normative sexual behavior involves a man depositing his seed in the woman or women he owns. The primacy of male genitals is established emphatically and early on in the first book of the Bible by God's covenant with the founding patriarch, Abraham:

> And God said to Abraham, "As for you, you shall keep my covenant, you and your descendants after you throughout their generations. This is my covenant, which you shall keep, between you and me and your descendants after you: Every male among you shall be circumcised. (Gen. 17:9-10)

Four verses follow in which the rite of circumcision is described and the "foreskin" is heralded as the "sign of the covenant between me and you . . . throughout your generations." Women are effectively eliminated from this fundamental covenant with God, and men are given the power and credit for procreating. Historian Gerda Lerner says:

> What is most striking is the omission of any symbolic or ritual role for the mother in the process of procreation. God blesses Abraham's seed as though it were self-generating. The image of the breast of the fertility-goddess nurturing the earth and the fields has been replaced by the image of the circumcised penis signifying the covenant contract between mortal men and God. Collective immortality in the form of many generations of children, land, power, and victory over their enemies is promised to the people of the covenant, if they fulfill their obligations, among which circumcision is primary.[35]

Sarah is an afterthought, mentioned later as the one by whom God will give a son to Abraham. She is kept ancillary, peripheral, and subordinate even in bearing children.

Throughout the Bible, four themes reinforce the centrality and superiority of men in procreative sexual ethics. These themes are (1) male lineage and genealogy, (2) the tragedy of "barren" women and the value of women as childbearers, (3) the use of "harlotry" as a metaphor for Israel's corporate sin, and (4) the wickedness of lesbians and gay men.[36] Together these themes pack a clear and powerful message that can be summarized as follows: Worthwhile women produce sons for men; when the Bible heralds the passing of generations, it does so by naming fathers and sons; when the Bible needs a metaphor for sin, it uses a woman's sexual rebellion against her master; when the Bible needs a scapegoat for wickedness, it uses those whose sexual practices are neither heterosexual nor procreative. Quite obviously the Bible is stacked in favor of heterosexual males ruling household, tribe, and nation; and a central factor in maintaining position is their control of sexual behavior.

Within such a patriarchal framework, therefore, lesbians and gay men should not be surprised to find passages that malign us. Our tendency, however, has been to apologize for those biblical passages that appear to condemn homosexuality and attack lesbians and gay men.

A LESBIAN/GAY READING OF THE BIBLE

During the past ten to twenty years many lesbian/gay Christians have attempted to reexamine and reread those passages that have traditionally been offered up as evidence that the Bible condemns us. We have questioned traditional interpretations, identified the heterosexism of biblical scholars, and searched for positive links between us and the Bible. Motivated by the hope that there might be a friendly voice for us in Scripture, we have searched for a neglected word or fact that would reverse or call into question traditional interpretations.

We have, for example, minimized the importance of Leviticus by noting the failure of Christians to adhere to many of its other prohibitions, not only the one prohibiting male homosexuality; we have also pointed to the cultural and cultic inappropriateness of the Levitical times for our own. We have argued that the sin of Sodom was not homosexuality, but rather inhospitality or gang rape. We have observed that Jesus said nothing about homosexuality, and that Paul was not critical of lesbians and gay men themselves, but of heterosexually oriented persons indulging in homosexual practices. Some have argued that the kind of homosexuality condemned in the

Bible is pederasty, not the loving, caring, consenting relationships between adults. Others have found in the Jonathan and David story and in the Naomi and Ruth story implications of intimacy, affection, and sexual love between people of the same gender.[37]

But in the interest of convincing ourselves and the church that the Bible does not condemn us, we have brought our own bias to our reading of it. We have tended to overlook the danger and hostility that lurk in the very passages with which we have tried to become friends. We have not been sufficiently skeptical of the patriarchal framework within which these passages occur. I would suggest that our approach to the Bible become less apologetic and more critical—that we approach it not as an authority from which we want approval, but as a document whose shortcomings must be cited.

To offer excuses for the Leviticus passage is to fail to grasp the seriousness with which our sexuality threatens patriarchy and the measures that those who benefit from patriarchy will take to secure and protect it:

> *You shall not lie with a male as with a woman; it is an abomination. (Lev. 18:22) If a man lies with a male as with a woman, both of them have committed an abomination; they shall be put to death, their blood is upon them. (Lev. 20:13)*[38]

Although some of us have said that this passage is but a single reference in a huge document that otherwise ignores us, I have to ask: "How many times and in how many ways do we have to be told that we should be killed before we take it seriously? Is not once enough?"

As a mere two lines of text this passage speaks with a clarity and precision that has sustained Christian patriarchy's condemnation of lesbians and gay men. The most recent examples in the arena of public policy-making are (1) the 1986 "Letter to the Bishops of the Catholic Church on the Pastoral Care of Homosexual Persons," written by the Congregation for the Doctrine of the Faith, with the approval of Pope John Paul II; and (2) the U.S. Supreme Court's

1986 *Bowers vs. Hardwick* decision. To justify church policy for excluding lesbian/gay people, the Congregation for the Doctrine of the Faith cites the passages from Leviticus:

> In *Leviticus* 18:22 and 20:13, in the course of describing the conditions necessary for belonging to the Chosen people, the author excludes from the People of God those who behave in a homosexual fashion.[39]

In holding that the constitutional right to privacy does not prevent states from criminalizing lesbian/gay sex, Chief Justice Warren Burger concurred with the majority opinion of the U.S. Supreme Court by noting that "the proscriptions against sodomy have very 'ancient roots'" and that "condemnation of such practices is firmly rooted in Judeo-Christian moral and ethical standards."[40]

But two other passages have been used as frequently against lesbians and gay men and are, indeed, texts of terror for us. One is the story of Sodom (Gen. 19) and the other is Paul's letter to the Romans (1:18-32). Both speak of us in terms that are inaccurate, vicious, bombastic, and alarmist. These passages are not unlike the lies and stereotypes that are heaped upon us today. They are not unlike the numerous movies and televisions dramas in which the criminal, drug-dealing, villainous, less-than-desirable characters are lesbian or gay.[41]

And just as I know that these modern media presentations do not accurately reflect our social behaviors, but instead try to reinforce a limited view of us, so the "wickedness" of the inhabitants of Sodom and their violent homosexual behavior are for me no longer stumbling blocks that I try to temper; they are lies that I name and for which I offer no apology. I place judgment on the passage and not on myself.

In the story of Sodom, two men (sometime referred to as "the two angels") are forced to defend themselves against attempted homosexual gang rape.

> Before [the two men] lay down, the men of the city, the men of Sodom, both young and old, all the people to the last man, surrounded the house; and they called to Lot: "Where are the men who came to

you tonight? Bring them out to us, that we may know them." Lot
went out of the door to the men, shut the door after him, and said,
"I beg you, my brothers, do not act so wickedly. Behold, I have two
daughters who have not known man; let me bring them out to you,
and do to them as you please; only do nothing to these men, for they
have come under the shelter of my roof." But they said, "Stand
back!" And they said, "This fellow came to sojourn, and he would
play the judge! Now we will deal worse with you than with them."
Then they pressed hard against the man Lot, and drew near to break
the door. But the [two] men put forth their hands and brought Lot
into the house to them, and shut the door. And they struck with
blindness the men who were at the door of the house, both small and
great, so that they wearied themselves groping for the door.
　　Then the men said to Lot, "Have you any one else here? Sons-
in-law, sons, daughters, or any one else you have in the city, bring
them out of the place; for we are about to destroy this place, because
the outcry against its people has become great before the Lord, and
the Lord has sent us to destroy it." (Gen. 19:4-14)[42]

It reads like a plot summary for the latest macho, sexist, rape-
and-pillage, straight-from-hell home video rental. And this fiction
is paradigmatic for the classic gay basher's defense that we often hear
today: "He made a sexual advance, so I had to beat or kill him."

In today's courts apprehended murderers of gay men are often
acquitted or given light sentences because the defendants claim that
the murdered victim made a sexual advance. The word of the
defendant is often sufficient to convince the court of real, imminent,
and otherwise unavoidable danger.[43] Although studies show that
"the majority of [public] homosexual solicitations are made only if
the other individual appears responsive and are ordinarily accom-
plished by quiet conversation and the use of gestures and signals
having significance only to other homosexuals,"[44] judges and jury
often assume that gay men are sexually violent and deserve to be
punished.

This legal defense is often given the kind of credibility in courts
of law that the Sodom story has received within the Christian

tradition. The story is an example of and support for the patriarchal privilege to fabricate a reason for attacking lesbians and gay men, to blame the victim. The preservers of patriarchy portray us as a wickedly violent, marauding people who need to be stopped; and in the Sodom story, stopping us is associated not only with self-defense and rightness, but with divine action, that is, self-defense by God's angels and destruction by God of the city. Make no mistake about the beneficiaries of patriarchy: they will go to the necessary extreme to embellish it and to discredit and remove us. The Sodom story stands in the tradition of such patriarchal propaganda.

Paul's letter to the Romans (1:18-32) is similarly vicious and misleading in its description of us. Within the space of eight verses (24-32), it says we "dishonor our bodies" and refers to "our dishonorable passions," "our shameless unnatural acts," "our base mind and improper conduct"; it says "we are filled with all manner of wickedness, evil, covetousness, malice, envy, murder, strife, deceit, malignity," that "we are gossips, slanderers, haters of God, insolent, haughty, boastful, inventors of evil, disobedient to parents, foolish, faithless, heartless, ruthless," and that we persist even though we know "God's decree that those who do such things deserve to die."[45]

Can there be any question as to what the writer and/or editor of this letter thinks of us? I am not convinced or soothed by claims that the letter targets a particular kind of homosexuality or that Paul attacks other kinds of sins, not just homosexuality, with the same enthusiasm. Biblical scholar Robin Scroggs's argument that the letter opposes "pederasty" and not consensual sexual relationships among adults is qualified by his own admission that "nothing in the language itself [in Rom. 1:26-27] would force one to limit its meaning to pederasty."[46] Scroggs also claims that the letter's charges are the kind of "catalog of vices" or "laundry list of evils" that was formulaic, "popular in Greco-Roman literature of the day," and generally used to discredit an opposing party in any dispute, and not constructed here specifically to oppose homosexuals.[47] But nowhere in the many times that they are used in Paul's letters is a list as extensive, accusatory, and singularly directed at particular behaviors. The full force of such lists to oppose and exclude emerges when same-sex relations are attacked. (Compare with Gal. 5:19-21; 1 Cor. 5:10-11; 1 Cor. 6:9- 10; 2 Cor. 12:20; Col. 3:5, 8; and Rom. 13:13.)[48]

It also makes little difference to me whether, as some scholars argue, Paul is against heterosexuals who violate their true nature by indulging in homosexuality or against homosexuals themselves; I do not feel that heterosexuals should be denied homoerotic experiences. What is important to see is that Paul associates turning away from God with same-gender erotic practices, i.e., that God gives up to same-gender sexuality those who turn away from him:[49]

> *For this reason God gave them up to dishonorable passions. Their women exchanged natural relations for unnatural, and the men likewise gave up natural relations with women and were consumed with passion for one another, men committing shameless acts with men and receiving in their own persons the due penalty for their errors.* (Rom. 1:26-27)[50]

Not to recognize, critique, and condemn Paul's equation of godlessness with homosexuality is dangerous. To remain within our respective Christian traditions and not challenge those passages that degrade and destroy us is to contribute to our own oppression. The 1986 "Letter to the Bishops of the Catholic Church" states:

> In Romans 1:18-32, still building on the moral traditions of his forbears, but in the new context of the confrontation between Christianity and the pagan society of his day, Paul uses homosexual behavior as an example of the blindness which has overcome humankind.[51]

Those passages will be brought up and used against us again and again until Christians demand their removal from the biblical canon or, at the very least, formally discredit their authority to prescribe behavior.

A BIBLICAL BASIS FOR LIBERATING SEXUALITY

Although these kinds of condemnations color the interpretation of sexuality in general and homosexuality in particular, there is nevertheless another voice within the Bible that, when explored, is very unlike the patriarchal sexual ethics dominating the other parts of the Bible and serves adequately to support a sexual ethics of giving and receiving body pleasure.[52] In "The Song of Songs," male dominance, female subordination, and stereotyping of either gender are absent. "Lover" and "friend" are synonymous; yearnings are not kept secret; all parts of the body are celebrated; woman is neither called wife nor required to bear children; procreation is not mentioned.[53] The following examples are selected passages from the Song:

> *How fine*
> *you are, my love,*
> *your eyes*
> *like doves'.*

> *How fine*
> *are you, my lover,*
> *what joy*
> *we have together.*

> *How green*
> *our bed of leaves*
> *our rafters of cedars,*
> *our juniper caves.*

> . . . .

> *My lover turns to me,*
> *I turn to him,*
> *Who leads his flock to feed*
> *Among the flowers.*

> . . . .

> My bride, my sister, I have come
> To gather spices in my garden,

To taste wild honey with my wine,
Milk and honey with my wine.

. . . .

Open, my love, my sister,
my dove, my perfect one,
for my hair is soaked with the night.

. . . .

Man of pleasure—sweet
To taste his love!
Friend and lover chosen
For my love.

. . . .

My love has gone to walk
Within his garden—
To feed his sheep and there
To gather flowers.

I turn to meet my love,
He'll turn to me,
Who leads his flock to feed
Among the flowers.[54]

In her new translation and interpretation of the Song, Hebrew scholar and poet Marcia Falk observes: "Women speak as assertively as men, initiating action at least as often; so, too, men are free to be as gentle, as vulnerable, even as coy as women. . . . Men and women are mutually praised for their sensual appeal and beauty."[55]

Although the Song is thoroughly heterosexual and leaves me still without any direct or explicit acknowledgment of my own sexuality, it seems *the* only part of the Bible with which we can form an alliance for constructing a sexual ethics based on the interests and needs of people for body pleasure. I would note, however, that this Song is but a few pages among a thousand, and it tends to be one of the most ignored books of the Bible.

Christian tradition, when it does pay it attention, has effec-tively allegorized, desexualized, abstracted, and interpreted this book so that its power to portray, encourage, and inspire lovemaking and body pleasure has been negated or flattened.[56] These intro-ductory remarks to "The Song of Solomon" by the editors of the Revised Standard Version of *The New Oxford Annotated Bible with Apocrypha* are an example:

> The Song has no overt religious content corresponding to that of the other books of the Bible, and can be interpreted only by assuming that a mystical symbolism is involved in its highly figurative language. Its inclusion in the Old Testament is to be explained from the pro-phetic figure of the LORD as the "husband" of his people (Hos. 2.16-19). In Christian tradition it has been interpreted as an alle-gory of the love of Christ for his bride, the church (Rev. 21.2,9), or as symbolizing the intimate experience of divine love in the individual soul.[57]

Falk argues that allegorical interpretations impose two main char-acters and a story line "on a text that seems instead to present a variety of voices speaking in a range of settings and without narrative sequence." What she sees as a collection of several types of lyric love poems has been forced to assume a structural unity that violates and obscures its diverse, sensual, "exquisitely rich imagery." She also detects "uneasiness, even embarrassment" among biblical scholars who find the various series of images describing parts of the human body "'comical,' 'puzzling,' 'bizarre,' 'grotesque.'" Traditional schol-arship and interpretation have conformed to and protected patri-archy from this possible threat—this "thoroughly nonsexist view of heterosexual love"—from within its own household and, conse-quently, have made constructing a sexual ethics of doing what is good, right, and pleasurable with our bodies a difficult task.[58]

The task is not made easier by Jesus' reported silence about "lesbians and gay men." I know that claiming "my ancestors" under such a modern umbrella term is problematic, if not outright fabrication. Michel Foucault has shown us that there is no monolithic, independent form of homoerotic expression or identity that traverses time and culture; but historian John Boswell has shown that there have always been persons self-conscious about their homoerotic desires.[59] Although cultural and historical recognition facilitates the development and expression of homoerotic attraction, we know that the feelings themselves are not dependent on or determined by such recognition.[60] I speculate (and own the personal bias and possible error of my speculation) that we have been in all places at all times, because as a boy growing up in a small rural town I felt and knew my affectional/sexual feelings and interests even though I did not have a name for them nor a culture in which or a people with which to practice them. Other lesbians and gay men recount similar experiences.[61] So I cannot imagine that we were not present on the streets of Galilee; and I do not take comfort from Jesus' apparent nonrecognition of us and inattention to our needs. Within the Judeo-Christian tradition, we have been a people who have learned to hide and be silent; we have survived often because we have not been recognized. And although that is precisely the kind of people that Jesus was able to reach and empower, we are not reported as those who touched him or were touched by him.

Jesus' ministry, to be sure, was remarkable; but it was not complete. Jesus is, for example, observed to have broken traditional barriers in his relationships with and regard for women; and yet his organization of twelve disciples was all male (as it has been recorded in the Bible[62]) and has provided a model for patriarchy that holds for structuring church leadership to this day.[63] We have the task of expanding and altering that ministry and of not accepting it as a finished product.

We perhaps have regarded Jesus too exclusively as a hero and not permitted him the status of friend who would value our criticism and contributions, regard the challenges we pose with greater interest than he would our obedience, and be made more aware and caring by our pain, dreams, and demands. If the ministry of Jesus is indeed to the needs and interests of people rather than in the service of the principalities of the social order, then we are needed to participate in and expand that ministry.

I do think, though, that we have from Jesus the encouragement to change that which is oppressive in our tradition and to break or repeal those rules, laws, and immoral lessons in the Bible that serve death and pain. When Jesus met a person with an injured hand on the Sabbath day, he was watched by the strict upholders of ceremony to see if he would break the Sabbath law and do the work of healing on that day. He looked at them with anger, grieved at their hardness of heart, and restored the person's hand.[64] So, also, does Erich Fromm tell us that in Jewish law "all commandments . . . are suspended when their observance might endanger life." He says: "Not only is it permissible to break these laws under such circumstances, but it is one's *duty* to break the law in order to save life."[65] Christians and Jews are obliged to end those practices and laws that dehumanize and cause the suffering and death of lesbians and gay men. And it is here that we may find our closest and most life-affirming link with Jesus to construct a sexual ethics that breaks with the dominant social order.

3

"And Vashti Refused":
Rewriting the Stories of the Silenced

A Role Model among Family Members

It was always a source of disappointment for me that I was not able to find a role model in the Bible—someone to identify with and admire, someone whose story had a special meaning for me, whose predicament or situation addressed the particularity of my own problems, concerns, and interests.

The range of biblical characters reminds me of that cast of characters that I grew up calling my family, that assortment of near and distant relatives who were variously falling in love, getting married, having children, gossiping about each other, going to war, raising children, getting into trouble, failing or succeeding at work, divorcing, and dying. It was the world into which I was born and it involved me totally whether I wanted it to or not.

As a child I participated in that world with the assumption that I would grow up to be like the others in it; as an adolescent I hoped, with increasing apprehension, that I would be able to find a place and fit into it; as a young adult I realized that what was important to me and what I wanted to do lay outside of it.

I have two distinct memories: One is that I never felt completely at home in this familial arrangement; although I did not know of an alternative that I would someday find and be in, I did feel that I did not really belong there. The other memory is of those numerous drives home from family get-togethers with me sitting in the back seat listening to my parents talking about who had been there. And it always seemed as though the one relative who had fascinated me and whose image was lingering pleasantly in my daydreams on the way home was the one whom my parents up in the front seat were criticizing because she wore too much rouge, too much jewelry, inappropriate clothing, was too loud or too casual, would never settle down, had wild ideas, or was too independent.

And it was this rather maverick and outlandish aunt, who seemed on the border of being in the family but not really of it, who was my secret role model, someone who affirmed the outsiderness I kept privatized, the one who seemed to be there for me, whether she knew it or not, but at the expense of being criticized and not entirely welcome.

Like the extended family in which I was raised, the biblical stories contain a range of characters and situations. And as one for whom Scripture had been a normative influence, I expected and wanted to find a personal, empowering connection to it. I have not been very successful, which is not to say that the stories are not powerful, important, and meaningful, any more than that certain relatives in my extended family have not played significant roles in my life. I am not saying that the Exodus, the prophetic call to make justice, or Jesus' ministry to the needy are not important or do not shape my outlook and behavior. But I am saying that among the variety of human experiences within my extended family and depicted in the Bible, my particular needs and dreams are not included. The themes and personal dynamics within both simply did not seem to have a place for the particular struggle within my own life. When I tried to identify with them, the connection was not direct and genuine. This, of course, has much to do with my being a gay man; but I have heard the same observation made by my students, all of them African-American men, in courses that I taught in a maximum-security prison; and women have made the observation as well.[1]

It is not without considerable effort that some of us have searched for a personally direct identification and link with Scripture. I have scoured and looked between the lines for the hidden messages of suppressed voices that might be uncovered to speak to me. But biblical stories revolve largely around the concerns and control of powerful men and those who serve them; and I am convinced now that to read them apologetically without criticism or protest is to allow myself to be flattened by them, to accommodate myself to them. Wanting or needing to find approval, understanding, a place, or connection within that huge document or within my extended family has often overshadowed for me the impact of being excluded from them. So, I have had to face the fact that if I find a link, a connection, to them, it must be found in recognizing and coming to terms with that exclusion.

A FEISTY, PUNISHED QUEEN

And yet, there *is* a snippet of a biblical story in which I find myself, in which I find a role model, someone to admire, get excited about, to root for, to model my behavior after. I hold her in the same esteem and regard her with the same fascination that I did my irregular aunt at those numerous family gatherings. For like my aunt, this biblical character does the unusual, is bold, defiant, disapproved of, and reprimanded.

One can easily miss or overlook the story of Queen Vashti. All of it is contained within a brief introduction to the Book of Esther. The following is my abridged telling of the story from chapter 1 of that book:

> *King Ahasuerus, who ruled from India to Ethiopia, gave a banquet for all his princes and servants, the army chiefs and the nobles and governors of the provinces under his rule. He showed them the riches of his royal glory and the splendor and pomp of his majesty for many*

days—180 days. And when this banquet was over, he gave another for those who lived in the capital city, a banquet lasting for seven days in the court of the garden of the king's palace. There were white cotton curtains and blue hangings attached by cords of linen and purple to silver rings and marble pillars; there were couches of gold and silver on mosaic floors of porphyry, marble, mother-of-pearl, and precious stones. Drinks were served in golden goblets, and the royal wine was lavished according to the bounty of the king.

Queen Vashti also gave a banquet for the women in the palace that belonged to King Ahasuerus. On the seventh day, when the king was merry with wine, he commanded his chamberlains to bring Vashti before him with her royal crown, in order to show the peoples and the princes her beauty; for she was fair to behold. But Queen Vashti refused to come at the king's command. At this the king was enraged; and his anger burned within him.

Then the king said to his wise men, who were versed in law and judgment, "According to the law, what is to be done to Queen Vashti, because she has not performed the command of the king?" And they responded, "Not only to the king has Queen Vashti done wrong, but also to all the princes and all the peoples in all the provinces of the king. For this deed of the queen will be made known to all women, causing them to look with contempt upon their husbands. If it please the king, let a royal order go forth from him, and let it be written among the laws that Vashti is to come no more before the king; and let the king give her royal position to another who is better than she. So when the decree made by the king is proclaimed throughout the land, all women will give honor to their husbands, high and low." This advice pleased the king; and the king did as they proposed.

In literary terms, Vashti's story is a device or vehicle to set the stage for the larger story of Esther. And even the Book of Esther itself is brief and is often overlooked and not recognized as important in the canon of Scripture. As a rather brief introduction to an otherwise brief and incidental book in Scripture, Vashti's story does not get top billing; so, I find my link, my connection, not in the well-known stories of the biblical tradition, but in a passage that is little known.

Queen Vashti is called away from socializing with her women friends to come before the king to show his visitors her beauty. But Vashti refuses to come; she seems to have preferred the company of her friends or had the good sense and self-respect not to appear before the drunken king as an object for display. Her refusal enrages the king, who turns to his wise men for advice. They claim that Vashti's actions have implications for the entire social order and, so, advise the king to dispose of Vashti and to proclaim throughout the land that all women give honor to their husbands—a striking and poignant illustration of patriarchal panic!

Esther is selected to replace Vashti, and Vashti disappears. Esther plays the role of queen quite differently. She strictly obeys the advice of her uncle Mordecai: she is an excellent student in the art of becoming lovely and beautiful in the eyes of important men. She uses her beauty to find favor with the king; and she prepares a sequence of dinners for him at which she eventually persuades him that her people are not being treated fairly. Her behind-the-scenes activity also gets her uncle Mordecai elevated to a position second only to the king.

LESSONS IN CONFORMITY AND OBEDIENCE

Vashti and Esther, of course, are a study in contrasts; and a lesson is obvious here about how women should behave and be effective. Literary scholar Eve Kosofsky Sedgwick observes:

Nothing is more explicit, in the Bible, about Esther's marriage than its origin in a crisis of patriarchy and its value as a preservative of female discipline. . . . Esther is introduced . . . as the salvific ideal of female submissiveness, her single moment of risk with the king given point by her customary pliancy. (Even today, Jewish girls are educated in gender roles—fondness for being looked at, fearlessness in defense of "their people," nonsolidarity with their sex—through masquerading as Queen Esther at Purim; I have a snapshot of myself at about five, barefoot in the pretty "Queen Esther" dress my grandmother made [white stain, gold spangles], making a careful eyes-down toe-pointed curtsey at [presumably] my father, who is

manifest in the picture only as the flashgun hurls my shadow, pillar-
ing up tall and black, over the dwarfed sofa onto the wall behind
me.)[2]

In simple terms, Vashti is the disobedient bad girl who is punished;
Esther is the heroine because she is obedient and knows how to
manipulate men without their knowing it. And this lesson is still
exemplified and taught at the highest levels of power.

Wifely obedience and sacrifice were probably no more clearly
displayed, rewarded, and celebrated than in the U.S. presidential
contest during the summer of 1992. Columnist Anna Quindlen
observes that the candidates' wives who got to speak at the national
conventions were Barbara Bush and Marilyn Quayle, "the women
behind the men," and asks, "Can you imagine the uproar if Hillary
Clinton had done the same?" She goes on to point out that Hillary
Clinton, an indepenent career woman as well as a wife and mother,
  was said to prefer the notion that two individuals together equaled
  two individuals. Folks said that made her an unnatural wife. . . .
  She couldn't give a speech at the Democratic Convention; people
  would have said she was ambitious and power mad, carrying . . .
  her own agenda.

Barbara Bush and Marilyn Quayle could speak at the Republican
Convention "because it's assumed they are there solely for their
men, altruism still considered more attractive than ambition in a
woman in some circles."[3]

You may also remember an incident in 1989 about which
Barbara Bush said in a interview "that she'absolutely' favored a ban
on weapons like the one used in the shooting . . . at a school in
Stockton, California, where five children were killed and more than
two dozen were wounded." President Bush, a lifetime member of the
National Rifle Association, on a previous occasion had said that he
did not favor a ban on such semiautomatic weapons because they are
typically used by sportsmen and hunters. A few days after Mrs.
Bush's interview, a *New York Times* headline read, "Barbara Bush

to Shun Public Stands on Issues," and the article followed with: "Barbara Bush decided to keep in the family disagreements with her husband on controversial issues after she and President Bush differed publicly over whether military-style assault weapons should be outlawed. Under a new policy disclosed [today], she will no longer talk publicly about things like gun control and abortion."[4]

The parallel with Vashti seems obvious. As soon as each woman speaks her own mind, disagrees publicly with her husband, acts thoughtfully and independently, she is reprimanded and silenced. The seriousness of the threat each poses to the social order is evidenced by the swiftness and efficiency with which new official policy is established and enforced. But the Bush incident also has parallels with Esther's part of the story, with the proper role of women exemplified by Esther's finding "favor in the king's eyes" and in her behind-the-scenes influence on public policy. Two weeks after the first article, we read that President Bush "softened his stance after lobbying by [William] Bennet [then director of national drug policy], by drug officers, and by his wife, Barbara."[5] After the officials and experts lent credence to her position, and after she had been silenced and placed behind the scenes, then the president could make his own decision.

SAVIORS AND BEARERS OF GOOD NEWS

You may be asking yourself, "What has this to do with finding good role models?" After all, is it not the point of these stories that Vashti is disposed of, Hillary Clinton silenced, and Barbara Bush rendered supportive? Where is the good news here? First of all, it is in the fact that they went against the normal flow of events, exercized independence, or spoke out at all. But more to the point is that the good news is not so much in the story itself as in our response to it, in how we rescue those who are punished, silenced, or reprimanded for acting like whole, independent human beings rather than obedient, nonthinking nonpersons. The good news is in our looking critically at, rather than automatically accepting as authoritative, the biblical document or the situations in which we find ourselves or into which we were born. Amidst the normal flow of events and under social pressure that are taken for granted, the good news is in saying, "Hey, wait a minute, the irregular aunt, the one that the family shunned because she did not conform, *she* is the one who saved my life; Vashti's refusal, not Esther's behind-the-scenes manipulations, is what encourages me to assert who I am and what I need; and Barbara Bush's direct perception and humane clarity offer a breath of fresh insight amid official rationalization and tolerance of recreational hunting and target practice with military-style assault rifles that fire an entire round of ammunition each time the trigger is pulled." The good news is that we find relief and salvation in the oddities and refusals of those people who are not normally taken seriously. But it is only good news if we can rescue their efforts from being silenced, trivialized, and broken further.

I am under no illusion about the meaning and purpose of Vashti's story as it appears in the Bible. It was not intended as a model for my or anyone else's liberation. Quite the opposite. In its context, it is a story about a woman who gets trashed for being strong. That she is disposed of is not meant to elicit sympathy or incite protest; if anything, it is a reminder of the cost of refusal and resistance. It is meant to frighten women and those who are expected to keep silent, to obey.

The good news is that we turn that story around, name it for what it is, bring attention to it. We counter the attempt to make this a brief reminder of what is unacceptable behavior and insist instead that Vashti's was a righteous action and an unjust punishment.

I would go even further and say the story is the occasion to reconsider the priority given to the various biblical stories and their significance to us. Just as there came a time in my personal life when I had to realize that what were valued as central and important events in my biological, extended family were not central and important to me, so I say also that even though Abraham, Noah,

David, Isaiah, Hosea, Jesus, and Paul are the recognized central and important figures in the Bible, for me they are not.

In lifting up her little-known or ignored story—in bringing it in from the margin to the center—in rewriting her story in our actions today, we use the Bible as a resource for moral agency, for making things better, for making justice. Instead of looking to the Bible for answers that can be copied to solve today's problems, instead of trying to copy what is done in the Bible, our confrontation with the Bible becomes a model for confronting the moral dilemmas we face in our lives today.

REWRITING VASHTI'S STORY

We can rewrite the story of Vashti because we are not looking for and do not expect the normal course of events to be sustaining and nurturing. We can rewrite Vashti's story because we know that answers and solutions to social problems are rarely found in the official word but can be constructed out of listening for and lifting up the silenced word. The story of Vashti has been rewritten many times, and we may continue to rewrite it.

The story of Vashti was rewritten when an underground railroad, and not complacency, was the response to a people's ignored cry for freedom; the story of Vashti was rewritten when armed resistance, and not accommodation, was the response to Hitler's program in the Warsaw Ghetto Uprising; the story of Vashti was rewritten when a boycott, and not continued obedience, was the response to the arrest of a tired woman who dared to sit down on a bus where she was not supposed to; the story of Vashti was rewritten when a few lesbians and gay men finally did not go gently into that ever-waiting paddy wagon outside the barroom door and staged the Stonewall Rebellion, the founding event of the modern lesbian/gay movement.[6]

The story of Vashti is rewritten in the hearing, the taking to heart, and the changes wrought when those who by saying no give us the power to yes. We cannot predict when such a voice will speak or when it will have the power to start a movement, raise consciousness, or change our lives. We only know that the voices usually come from the margins, from those who are not usually taken seriously, from those desperate enough to see clearly. But we can place ourselves in their midst; we do not have to place our faith in the normal course of events or in the word from on high; we do have the option of listening to the voices from below and outside.

One of those voices spoke to us during the much-publicized gang rape of a young professional white woman by adolescent men of color in New York City's Central Park in the spring of 1990. Attention to the different race and class of victim and perpetrators and criticism of the woman's practice of jogging alone at night in a public park often obscured the issue of sexual violence against women. Some suggested that the prosecution of the socially less-advantaged perpetrators was biased and unduly aggressive because of the woman's race and privileged economic status. Others thought she put herself in danger by choosing to exercise in an area frequented by street-smart boys socialized and prone to violent behavior. Actually, the boys were from a variety of backgrounds.[7] Joan Morgan, a woman of color, dared to deal with the complexity and divisiveness of these issues as the assault became spectacularized in the news media. Before, during, and after the trial, the victim herself was never named, did not speak, and remained in protected seclusion to recover from the near-fatal assault. Morgan rewrote the woman's story in her own and others' stories:

> Some who knew her have suggested that she was simply not the type to be hedged in by limitations or to accept being told that she could not do something because she was female. I can dig that. I know women like that. Sisters who refuse to internalize the filth, to turn themselves inside themselves. To hide their beauty and their brownness in an effort not to be noticed. Women who still . . . choose to walk down male-owned streets wearing miniskirts and flaunting shapely, strong legs. Who dare to put bright red lipstick on full lips. Some of us fight because losing the sensuous fullness of our identity

is too painful a sacrifice. Some of us fight because we've been doing it so long we've simply forgotten how not to.

I guess we're crazy, too. We can be likened to the crazier brothers and sisters who refused 30 years ago to walk down southern streets yes ma'aming and no suhing. The ones who absolutely refused to step off the curb when white people chose to walk on the same side of the street. The ones who still opened up businesses and went to hate-filled white schools. Like them, we silently bear our scars, and we stand in the face of lynch mobs—whose color, sometimes, is the same as our own.[8]

Morgan rewrites Vashti's story not in those acts of resistance that have become publicly commemorated and championed but in those moments of refusal and assertiveness in everyday life when we choose not to swallow the lump in our throat, when we speak out, push on, and do the unexpected so that we can survive and live more fully. She tells the story in terms of those moments that go unnoticed by the media but are special and important for preserving and building a person's dignity, pride, and worth.

AN EVERYDAY STORY

Morgan's words and Vashti's story are lost if we do not recognize them in the everyday, personal aspects of our own lives. If we see them as other people's stories, as removed from and more heroic than what we ourselves do and can do, then Vashti remains an insignificant victim in an incidental chapter to a short story about the merits of obedience and passive manipulation. When we listen to and lift up the voice within us that is too easily avoided and silenced by the seemingly more important demands of others around us, Vashti lives and so do we.

To be sure, we cannot refuse, resist, and assert ourselves completely at all times, at every obstacle. Sometimes an incident or the moment presents choices with clarity and immediacy, and we choose to act promptly or to delay for a safer or more advantageous time. Often, only after enduring and conforming to common practice and expectations, we see alternatives, make decisions, act.

For several years now my lover and I have been invited to the full range of my biological family's gatherings—weddings, silver and golden wedding anniversaries, Thanksgiving and Christmas holidays. We attend with appreciation for being included as a gay couple and with a feeling of responsibility to be who we are, especially for my nephews and niece, one of whom has told us he is gay. But my lover and I have also admitted to each other that we attend these gatherings mostly out of duty, obligation, and gratitude rather than because they are especially meaningful or enjoyable. The only holidays we celebrate together with gift giving and special food are Valentine's Day, our own anniversary, and our birthdays.

This year when my mother and I went out to buy her Christmas tree, she asked how we would be decorating our house for the holidays. I paused for moment, took a breath, and explained that Christmas (and Chanukah, since my lover is Jewish) is not very important for us and that we choose not to celebrate the traditional holidays on our own. A few moments passed, and unprompted she asked if we observe and celebrate an anniversary of our relationship. I said that we do. She asked if it is the anniversary of when we first met, started living together, or . . . uh. And I finished for her: "Made love? No. It's of the day we met." Some silent, thought-filled moments passed before we got to the tree market. I would bet my life that my lover and I will be receiving our first happy anniversary card from her this year.

4

Lessons from Leviticus:
Learning about the Misuse of Power

WHY READ IT AND ITS PLACE IN THE BIBLE

IF WE THINK OF THE BOOK OF LEVITICUS at all, it is usually as that rather tedious part of the Bible with the seemingly endless lists of regulations about different ways to prepare sacrifices, what not to eat, what not to wear, and how not to have sex. We usually lift out the two nice verses about loving neighbor and stranger and dismiss the rest as out of step with life as we know it today.

You shall not hate your brother in your heart, but you shall reason with your neighbor, lest you bear sin because of him. You shall not take vengeance or bear any grudge against the sons of your own people, but you shall love your neighbor as yourself: I am [Yahweh].

When a stranger sojourns with you in your land, you shall not do him wrong. The stranger who sojourns with you shall be to you as the native among you, and you shall love him as yourself; for you were strangers in the land of Egypt: I am [Yahweh] your God. (Lev. 19:17-18, 33-34)[1]

But there is another dimension to Leviticus that we have perhaps not considered seriously enough; and it may be a helpful

61

resource for understanding current social conditions and how to cope with them. I want to look at those parts of Leviticus that we find offensive, objectionable, and wrong.

First, though, we should be clear about the place and role of Leviticus in the biblical canon. It is the third of the first five books of the Bible, often called the Pentateuch or Five Books of Moses. Although compiled and written at various times and places and by a variety of people, the books and the various stories within them are arranged to form a continuous narrative history of Israel, from creation and the founding patriarchs to entering the promised land. The narrative theme and historical concern are different in each book:

1. The Book of Genesis, with its narrative theme of the promise to the patriarchs, is concerned with primeval history and the history of the patriarchs.
2. The Book of Exodus, with its narrative theme of the exodus from Egypt, is concerned with the crucial event in Israel's history: its deliverance from slavery by Yahweh.
3. The Book of Leviticus, with its narrative theme of the sojourn at Sinai, is concerned with instituting the rules of worship and daily life, the duties of priests, and familial land tenure after the future arrival in the promised land.
4. The Book of Numbers, with its narrative theme of guidance in the wilderness, is concerned with the census and ordering of Israel's families.
5. The Book of Deuteronomy, with its narrative theme of guidance to the Promised Land, is concerned with planning for centralizing worship in one place.

Unlike the other books, Leviticus is less of a story and more of a collection of statutes, ordinances, laws, and commandments spoken by Yahweh to those gathered as Sinai.[2]

I first began studying Leviticus because it prescribes death for male homosexuality and yet welcomes and loves the neighbor and stranger.

You shall not lie with a male as with a woman; it is an abomination. (Lev. 18:22)

If a man lies with a male as with a woman, both of them have committed an abomination; they shall be put to death, their blood is upon them. (Lev. 20:13)[3]

These two verses may seem small and insignificant in a book of 859 verses. Even the lists of other sexual offenses, of which these two verses are a part, are neither numerically significant nor a major theme in Leviticus. Also, in Leviticus the penalty of death is not limited to male homosexuality; other such punishable behaviors are cursing parents, adultery, incest, marrying both a woman and her mother, bestiality, wizardry, harlotry, working on the Sabbath, cursing the name of Yahweh, and murder.[4] Nonetheless, the gravity of capital punishment, even if mentioned only once and not limited to homosexuality, provoked my serious attention, especially because for our own times prescribing both death for gay men as well as love for the stranger seems contradictory. How can one both love and kill those who are other, marginal, outsiders, strangers?[5]

But a closer examination of Leviticus shows that the Hebrew term for sojourner or stranger (*ger*) is more accurately translated as "resident alien," one who was born elsewhere but has the economic means to live and work as an accepted member and according to the standards of the community. The term for neighbor (*rea'*) also means companion, brother, fellow countryman, one of one's own. To love neighbors and sojourners in Leviticus is to love those who are closest to and most like oneself; the condition for communal love here is homogeneity, not outreach to the margins of society. Regulations concerning foreigners or outsiders use other terms (*zar* and *ben-neykar*) and do not express welcome but deny access to certain communal and cultic practices.[6]

EXCLUSIVITY, SUPERIORITY, AND PROTECTION

One looks in vain for an example of inclusive community, egalitarian principles, or a theology of loving outreach and pluralistic justice in Leviticus. The term *qadash*, meaning "set apart" and "holy," occurs 152 times in Leviticus (20 percent of all occurrences in Hebrew Scripture).[7] As the following passage shows, Leviticus is about defining a separate community by establishing its superior differences from others:[8]

> *You shall therefore keep all my statutes and all my ordinances, and do them; that the land where I am bringing you to dwell may not vomit you out. And you shall not walk in the customs of the nation which I am casting out before you; for they did all these things, and therefore I abhorred them. But I have said to you, "You shall inherit their land, and I will give it to you to possess, a land flowing with milk and honey." I am the Lord your God, who have separated you from the peoples. You shall therefore make a distinction between the clean beast and the unclean. . . . You shall be holy to me; for I [Yahweh] am holy, and have separated you from the peoples, that you should be mine. (Lev. 20:22-26)*[9]

The great number of regulations about worship and daily life in Leviticus delineate precisely who may be inside and who will be put outside of the community and who, in its own terms, will be "cut off from their people."[10]

The above passage occurs at the end of the section in which death is prescribed for male homosexuality (20:13), and a similar introduction and summary (18:1-5,24-30) frame the section containing the other prohibition of homosexuality (18:22). Antihomosexuality would appear to have been part of the community's effort to separate and distinguish itself. Elsewhere and throughout Leviticus, the privileging of a priesthood of "unblemished," married heterosexual males,[11] the inferiority of the female gender in sacrifices and ceremonies,[12] and measures protecting sexual ownership of women by men[13] reinforce exclusivity, hierarchy, and patriarchy.

In its social, as well as sexual and cultic legislation, Leviticus mandates mutual support among those who are insiders. Concern for the poor, widows, and orphans, a theme recurring throughout Jewish and Christian Scripture, is absent in Leviticus, replaced by concern for oneself and those within one's familial organization—

for "your brother [blood relative], if he should become poor" (25:25, 35, 45). A comparison of the different wording in Exodus and Leviticus of the law to let the fields lie fallow every seventh year also shows the self-interest of Leviticus. In Exodus 23:11 the fields are to lie fallow so that "the poor of your people and . . . the wild beasts may eat," whereas in Leviticus 25:6-7 "the sabbath of the land shall provide food for you, for yourself and for your male and female slaves and for your hired servant and the sojourner who lives with you; for your cattle also and for the beasts that are in your land."[14] Another provision in Leviticus, the proclamation of a Jubilee Year or Year of Release, is often heralded by modern social justice advocates as an inspiration or model for economic reform:

> You shall hallow the fiftieth year, and proclaim liberty throughout the land to all its inhabitants; it shall be a jubilee for you, when each of you shall return to his property and each of you shall return to his family. (Lev. 25:10)[15]

But the provision's purpose in Leviticus and for the times in which it was written is "property-restitution" and "bankruptcy law" for the landowning class; it "is essentially an effort to hold the [patriarchal] family together."[16]

WRITTEN FOR WHAT PURPOSE?

We need to ask under what conditions such a document was written and compiled. What kind of document or social situation requires the kind of prescriptions, conditions, and punishment cited above? Why was it written as it was written?

Leviticus was shaped by two events: (1) the fall of Jerusalem and the subsequent forced removal or exile of its upper class to Babylon, and (2) forty-nine years later, the decree by Cyrus, the Persian emperor who conquered Babylon, to allow the exiles to return.[17] Leviticus is a document that describes, interprets, and reframes Israel's ancient sojourn at Sinai according to the needs of the postmonarchical present.[18]

The dispersion or exile to Babylon was "a forced removal of royalty, state officials, priests, army officers, and artisans who probably constituted no more than 5 percent of the total populace." The edict of Cyrus allowed them to return. This was part of a wider policy of extending to certain subject people considerable autonomy and respect for their indigenous cultural and religious life when such was an advantage to the Persian empire. It was to Cyrus's advantage to prevent a weak point of defense in the empire's west by stabilizing Jerusalem and the surrounding province of Judah. The exiles were allowed to return on the condition that they support and conform to the authority of the Persian empire. Israel could be restored, but only as a *religiously* autonomous, politically *dependent* community.[19]

Returning to establish a ruling religious elite was one of the few options open to the Babylonian exiles if they wanted to regain some measure of their former position and wealth.

They came back to find towns and villages destroyed, Jerusalem largely in ruins, despair and poverty common. They had the added task of trying to control a land that had been open to the influx of neighboring peoples and the tendency of natives to adopt the social and religious customs of foreigners. "To differentiate Israel as a distinct people with its own peculiar marks of circumcision, Sabbath, food laws, festivals, and sacrifices" was "a *stabilizing strategy*" during "the profound shock that Israel underwent in the transition from political independence to colonial servitude."[20]

Leviticus attempts to reinterpret the history of Israel in favor of these new developments. An important event in Israel's ancient history—the sojourn at Sinai—is remembered, reshaped, and used as the historical precedent for consolidating and controlling Israel's postexilic religious community. Cultic practices, sexual and social regulations, and the organization of priests are reformalized and presented as the words Yahweh spoke to Moses at Sinai.

The desperation to grab and institutionalize control is evident in the exaggerated detailing of regulations, the severity of punishments, and the bullying language that frames them. Nowhere else in Hebrew Scripture, for example, are sexual laws and prescriptions of death for them as numerous,[21] nor is the otherwise rare phrase "I am Yahweh" used so often to infuse laws with imposing and frightening authority.[22]

Understanding the Motive

This emphasis on precisely controlling personal behavior when faced with diminishing or limited national power may be instructional and applicable for us today. Instead of selectively rejecting or accepting certain rules in Leviticus according to our current values, we may try to understand the rules as the response by a particular class of people to the social conditions of its time. Should we be surprised that a formerly powerful ruling class would separate, protect, reward, and establish itself with whatever power and authority were available to it? And since politics and economics on the national and international levels were in the hands of an outside government, should we be surprised that local law and order efforts turned to legislating sexual, social, and religious behaviors and protecting the property of local landowners?

To understand this response, however, is not to approve of it. To understand the words and actions of a " 'declassed' elite" trying to regain social stability[23] is not meant to garner sympathy for those efforts. Rather, such understanding brings into sharper focus the basis and consequence of its social and religious policy. We come to see, for example, that the prohibitions of homosexuality are not odd bits of nastiness but an integral part of an entire program in which a few people make strict rules and threaten to exclude, kill, or severely punish those who do not obey them. When compared with the rules in other books of the Bible, these rules are less humanitarian and more punitive, the superiority of men and their sexual ownership of women are more pronounced, and the language is more bombastic and intimidating.

The lesson that emerges from this understanding of Leviticus is as follows: When those favored by patriarchy are stripped of power and privilege, their subsequent efforts to regain or maintain some measure of control exaggerate and nearly caricature patriarchy in reduced spheres of influence. General assumptions and practices underlying patriarchy are finely tuned into specific laws: disapproval of homosexuality becomes a law against and punishment of it; and male dominance denied in the political arena is shifted to and reaffirmed in explicit laws about sex and worship. This compensatory, extremist, and selective micromanagement of the social order may have some direct application to social conditions and decision making in our own institutions today.

A SIMILAR SITUATION?

I do not want to suggest that there is an exact parallel between social conditions in postexilic Israel and the current United States. But there are similarities that may help us to see our times more clearly. I am thinking, of course, of the United States' decline in economic growth and international power and the increased polarization of its social classes and groups:

1. During the 1980s, the shift in fiscal policy from one of tax-and-spend to one of spend-and-borrow more than doubled federal indebtedness. The government sold assets to and borrowed from foreign investors and now owes nearly one-half of the rapidly increasing debt to foreign lenders. Until 1981 the United States had been "a net creditor country and increasingly so"; the new "policy has transformed us from a creditor to a debtor" nation. "World power and influence have historically accrued to creditor countries"; Japan and West Germany have now emerged as the world's largest creditors.[24]

2. As "the reduction of American incomes required to restore international equilibrium" occurs, the effect will be harsher than ever before "because it will take place in the context of little real growth." In addition to "handing over our assets to foreigners to service our debt," the "new fiscal

policy has left a lower stock of productive capital and therefore a lower level of productivity than we otherwise would have had."[25] "From 1973 to 1990 output per hour grew by 0.9 in the U.S.," while neither Canada, France, Germany, Italy, France, nor Great Britain "scored below 20 percent."[26]

3. From 1973 to 1991 "the real (inflation-adjusted) hourly wage for nonsupervisory workers" fell "(with little interruption) almost 13 percent"; with the exception of the U.S., "no other First World country has seen an outright protracted decline" in real wages. Also, the U.S. now has "the smallest middle class and the highest poverty rates in the First World."[27]

4. Typically, during periods of economic decline, difficulties do not fall equally on all people.[28] "Income distribution, which had been growing less unequal from the time of the New Deal until the late 1960s, started growing more unequal sometime in the early 1970s." Not only have the rich gotten richer, and the poor gotten poorer and more numerous, but "income distribution among African Americans, always more unequal than among whites, has grown even more lopsided over the last couple of decades," and "among women, the gap between well- and poorly-paid has widened, too."[29]

5. When standards of living plummet, especially unequally among groups, conflicts and boundaries between groups sharpen.[30] "As the society polarized, and the frustrations of having to work harder just to stay in place deepened, the political atmosphere grew steadily nastier. . . . It became increasingly popular to blame welfare mothers, drugged sociopaths, and the Japanese for our problems. The failings of the investing and managing classes have gone largely unexamined."[31]

6. The most affluent manage to save themselves and prosper. By becoming "more and more integrated into the global

economy, they become more and more divorced from
those Americans they are leaving behind. . . . It is, in
market terms, more efficient to buy Korean, Taiwanese, or
mainland Chinese workers."[32]

The following tentative parallels can be suggested between the times
of Leviticus and those of today:

The economic shift and the loss of the Vietnam War in the
early 1970s signaled a decline in the United States' international
standing that may be compared to the fall of Israel's monarchy.
Although the U.S. ruling class was not subject to the equivalent of
exile, the government has become financially indebted to and
dependent on investment by foreign businesses. The so-called
boom and expansion of the 1980s, in which "60% of the income
gains . . . went to the upper one percent of the income distribution," was at the expense of growing federal indebtedness—perhaps
not unlike the safekeeping of exiles in Babylon while Judah was in
ruins and the people remaining there were ignored, grew poor, and
became despondent.

And just as Cyrus allowed the exiles to return to stabilize Judah
as a religious community and maintain peace in a troubled part of
the Persian empire, so have the major economic powers of the world
allowed the United States to maintain military autonomy in order
to stabilize international relations for prospering industrial countries. Neither the United States nor postexilic Israel is restored to
its former status; instead, a prominent national characteristic of each
(religion or military) is encouraged and used to the advantage of
those who have economic and political power. Each enthusiastically
embraces the opportunity to maintain some measure of autonomy
and power and lets what was a national characteristic *define* the
nation.

The enthusiasm and bombast with which Leviticus demonstrates its religious authority are not unlike the United States'
celebrated military victories over tiny countries like Panama and
Grenada or its televised live coverage of computerized, surgical

bombings and mass destruction in the Gulf War. But beyond mere posturing and boasting, both also realize the economic advantage of their new roles: Leviticus writes into Yahweh's words provisions for land return and bankruptcy protection for the ruling class; and, having used the Gulf War as a worldwide showroom for the most advanced military technology, the United States effectively moves to the forefront in selling arms to Third World countries and increases its control of international conflict and aggression.

Each, also, when denied its former national status and international role, turns to controlling sexual and personal behaviors and punishing deviance and difference with unprecedented attention. The comparison of the laws in Leviticus with the fewer, vaguer, and more humanitarian laws in Exodus has already been made. A similar one can be made by observing the third and fourth quarters of the present century in the United States.

Looking at Our Times

In the decade following World War II, the tightening of patriarchal reins—as reflected in public policy reestablishing the family as nuclear, returning women from the paid work force to unpaid housework, defining men as providers for the household, and formalizing the repression of political and sexual "deviance" in the form of the McCarthy hearings and patriotism—was instrumental in gearing up the United States for dominance in world affairs. As the country became established as a primary world power, however, its social order could tolerate more, exclude less, and define itself more broadly because its position was not threatened or uncertain.

Concurrent with the post-World-War-II rise to international power and domestic prosperity from the mid-1950s to the mid-1970s was the emergence of increased human rights and protection for sexual freedom.

In 1954 and 1955 in *Brown v. Board of Education*, the U.S. Supreme Court required the desegregation and integration of public schools. In 1965 in *Griswold v. Connecticut*, the court ruled that a married couple had the right of privacy to choose contraception; in 1972 in *Eisenstadt v. Baird*, this right was extended to the individual; and in 1973 in *Roe v. Wade*, it was extended further to a woman's right to choose abortion.[33]

During this same period the U.S. Congress passed the 1964 Civil Rights Act, the 1967 Age Discrimination in Employment Act, the 1968 Fair Housing Act, and the 1973 Rehabilitation Act, together barring discrimination based on race, national origin and ethnicity, gender, religion, age, and disability.

Among religious denominations and organizations, in 1969 the United Church of Christ published the first collection of church-related essays by lesbians and gay men, and in 1972 it ordained into Christian ministry the first openly gay man. In 1972 the San Francisco Board of Rabbis voted to support legalizing any private sexual acts between consenting adults; and in 1973 the United Association of Hebrew Congregations accepted for membership a newly formed, predominantly lesbian/gay Los Angeles temple. In 1970 in a Catholic clerical journal, the Jesuit priest John McNeill questioned church teaching on extramarital sex and defended stable homosexual relationships; and in 1973 the National Federation of Priests' Council officially commissioned a gay task force to develop a model for extending Christian ministry to homosexual people.[34]

Social movements by people of color, students, women, and lesbian/gay people became visible and took form during this period of economic prosperity and international status.

Signaling the retrenchment and eventual cancellation of these permissions and humanitarian accomplishments are the following developments in the late 1970s and 1980s:

Several decisions by the U.S. Supreme Court have shifted from protecting human rights and sexual freedom.[35] While the court had consistently interpreted new civil acts broadly through the 1960s, the first restrictive ruling was issued in 1975 with others to follow.[36] In 1989 the court "handed down seven decisions that restrictively interpreted provisions of the 1866 and 1964 Civil Rights Acts that prohibit employment discrimination."[37] In 1986 the court limited the right of privacy in *Bowers v. Hardwick* by upholding the constitutionality of Georgia's law against consensual sodomy;[38] and in a series of other decisions, restrictions have been placed on a woman's right to have an abortion.[39]

In 1983 the U.S. Congress defeated the proposed Twenty-seventh Amendment to the Constitution, the Equal Rights Amendment.[40] A bill introduced in 1975 to amend the Civil Rights Act to prohibit discrimination based on affectional or sexual preference has never been passed. Proposed legislation for lesbian/gay rights on state and other municipal levels during the past twenty years have been met with contention, delay, passage, repeal, defeat, and counter-legislation.[41] For example:

> *Springfield, Ore., became the first town in modern U.S. history to mandate discrimination against gay men and lesbians when, on May 19 [1992], citizens voted to outlaw civil rights for gay people. The vote, 5,693 to 4,540, bans gay pride events from public property, among other things.*
>
> *Under the law, any city agency may deny services to gay social, political and religious organizations, as well as nongay groups that support civil rights for gay people. Public libraries will be required to remove from their shelves any items that treat homosexuality in a positive or neutral manner. The measure also proactively bans the city from passing or enforcing any law that recognizes sexual orientation.*
>
> *Voters in Corvallis, Ore., rejected an identical measure, 4,486 to 8,048.*[42]

Seven states—Wisconsin, Massachusetts, Hawaii, Connecticut, New Jersey, California, and Vermont—have passed some form of lesbian/gay rights legislation. In New York a bill has been proposed and allowed to die in the state legislature for twenty-one consecutive years. Referenda results during the 1992 elections capture the mixture of victory and defeat for rights legislation: Voters in Oregon rejected a statewide measure that would allow discrimination and denounce homosexuality as abnormal and perverse, whereas Colorado voters passed a statewide ban on antidiscrimination laws that protect lesbians and gay men. Voters in Portland, Maine, rejected a measure to repeal its local lesbian/gay rights ordinance, but voters in Tampa, Florida, did repeal their ordinance.[43]

Among religious denominations, the United Methodist church in 1976 adopted a resolution prohibiting the ordination of openly lesbian/gay people. The United Presbyterian Church, USA (UPC), and the Episcopal church followed suit. Decisions at subsequent denominational meetings in the 1980s and 1990s reaffirmed these bans. In 1976 the Rabbinical Assembly of the Conservative Judaism decided without explanation that separate lesbian/gay congregations should not be established. In 1986 the Vatican's Congregation for the Doctrine of the Faith issued a document to halt the growing pro-gay movement among Catholics; the letter restated traditional Catholic teaching that homosexual behavior is an "intrinsic moral evil" and banned any group that disagreed from meeting on church property. In a 1992 statement the Vatican strengthened its position by explicitly condoning in unprecedented detail discrimination against homosexuals in adoptions, foster care placements, military service, and employment of teachers and athletic coaches. In 1988 the Southern Baptist Convention condemned homosexuality as an abomination in the eyes of God and has since expelled two local churches for blessing same-sex unions and licensing a gay candidate for ministry. In 1991 the American Baptists voted to condemn homosexuality as a sin, and the Christian Church (Disciples of Christ) voted not to elect Michael K. Kinnamon as its president because of his liberal views on homosexuality. Unlike all previous nominations by administrative committee to the General Assembly, Kinnamon was the first not to be elected. In 1992 the highest court of the Presbyterian Church (USA) overruled two lower courts to nullify the hiring of openly lesbian Rev. Jane Adams Spahr by a church in Rochester, New York. The United Association of Hebrew Congregations, Reconstructionist Judaism, United Church of Christ, Friends, and Unitarian Universalist Association have continued to support officially lesbian/gay people; but these organizations have not been without internal opposition, controversy, and setbacks.[44]

As the liberal social agenda of the sixties and early seventies has deteriorated amid the economic and international instability of the late seventies, eighties, and early nineties, the prevailing topics of public discourse during this shift have been affirmative action, abortion, and homosexuality.[45] Presidential, congressional, and state election campaigns have been shaped, lost, and won by the positions and packaging of candidates on these issues. Debate of these issues has repeatedly dominated the national conventions of religious bodies.

This apparent fascination with not wanting to "overfavor" the poor, with controlling the bodies of women, and with prohibiting the sexual behavior and acceptance of lesbian/gay/bisexual people is especially macabre in the context of the United States' ever-widening gap between rich and poor, the loss of economic productivity, and the depths of poverty to which an unprecedented number of people have sunk. It is intriguing, ironic, and tragic, as well, that over the past decade the kind of social legislation that has been frequently and easily passed and that has been pervasively implemented has to do with controlling the behavior of tobacco smokers, whereas legislation to help the poor and stabilize the economy has been piecemeal and ineffective. No legislation in health care, education, and housing has been passed that comes close to the comprehensive reach and effectiveness of antismoking regulations and policy.

That so much attention has been devoted to abortion and homosexuality might not be so distressing if the opinion of the majority of people had informed and influenced the decisions that legislators, judges, and other leaders have made about them. "In poll after poll following *Hardwick*, it was clear that the majority of Americans found [sodomy] laws repugnant."[46] Surveys also show that most people support a woman's right to abortion and disapprove of discrimination against lesbian/gay people; and yet public policy decisions have not in most instances adhered to the public's wishes.[47]

It should also be noted that a Harris Survey in 1982 showed that 73 percent of the adult population favored the Equal Rights Amendment.[48]

The privileged and powerful minority's disregard for majority consensus, indifference to the disadvantaged, control of women, opposition to deviation from male heterosexual dominance, and codification of daily behaviors seem not unlike the hierarchy, homogeneity, and exclusivity put forth in Leviticus. And although we may understand that when the powerful are threatened they will cling to and exaggerate the power remaining to or allowed them, we must find a way to insist on equal distribution of power, diversity, and inclusivity.

RESOURCES FOR EQUALITY, DIVERSITY, AND INCLUSIVITY

The generosity that the powerful can afford during economic prosperity and stability dries up as a resource for change in less stable times. Just as we cannot now look to and rely on them for permission and help in building a just and inclusive community, we cannot look to Leviticus as an authority, model, or example. Nor can we simply dismiss either of these as if they do not exist. A head-on look at our current social situation and at Leviticus jolts us out of an unconditional acceptance of our established leaders and of the Bible. We are compelled to weigh and evaluate, to identify what is oppressive and liberative in our biblical tradition and in our current lives, to lift up what is at the heart of the Bible.

In "ascertaining the original elements" and major themes of the Pentateuch, biblical scholarship shows that the deliverance from slavery in Exodus "has the greater weight and thus the right to be accorded priority"; "the narratives of the sojourn in the wilderness [in Leviticus] treat a theme which is subordinate and dependent, because it needs to lean on major themes both before and after." Our reading of the Bible should recognize that within the Pentateuch the Exodus, not the sojourn at Sinai, is the primary event on which all others depend, and that throughout the Bible "one of the most fundamental and frequently repeated statements of faith . . . is that Yahweh . . . is the one who 'led Israel out of Egypt.'"[49]

The Book of Exodus tells of the deliverance from slavery in Egypt, with repeated emphasis on the oppression, affliction, physical hardship, and suffering of the slaves.[50] Yahweh's well-known words to Moses are:

> I have seen the affliction of my people who are in Egypt, and have heard their cry because of their taskmasters; I know their sufferings, and I have come down to deliver them out of the hand of the Egyptians. (Exod. 3:7-8a)[51]

We find our anchor in and take strength from the priority given those who suffer in Exodus, rather than from those who control and exclude in Leviticus. "The belief in the deliverance from Egypt belonged to the oldest and most universal heritage of the Israelite tribes";[52] we claim that heritage as our own and put it to work for us here today.

We listen to and build community with those who are not meant to survive. We find our meaning, our God, not in the image of the finger-shaking, boastful one who separates and scolds us, who calls us to scurry for whatever bit of advantage we can grasp and hold against another; rather, we find meaning in the cry of the voices from the outside, from those who have been cut off, excluded, such as this one:

> As a forty-nine-year-old Black lesbian feminist socialist mother of two, including one boy, and a member of an interracial couple, I usually find myself part of some group defined as other, deviant, inferior, or just plain wrong. . . .
>
> Institutionalized rejection of difference is an absolute necessity in a profit economy which needs outsiders as surplus people. . . . As a result, those differences have been misnamed and misused in the service of separation and confusion.
>
> Certainly there are very real differences between us of race, age, and sex. But it is not those differences between us that are separating us. It is rather our refusal to recognize those differences, and to

examine the distortions which result from our misnaming them and
their effects upon human behavior and expectation. . . .
    Change means growth, and growth can be painful. But we
sharpen self-definition by exposing the self in work and struggle
together with those whom we define as different from ourselves,
although sharing the same goals.[53]

We find our meaning, we image our God, in the cry of an African-American lesbian who is "trying to become the strongest person I can become, to live the life that I have been given and to help effect change toward a liveable future for this earth and for my children," and who wants, invites us, to do that with her, and who insists that her pain and wishes are not more or less important than our own.[54]

    We continue or begin yet again to be a people who find their meaning in gathering to make peace and justice, to give and receive nurture, to find sustenance, to welcome the outsider. We continue to take seriously those who are not otherwise taken seriously.

    Just as the Book of Leviticus does not represent the concerns of the many who faced the conditions of those times, the decisions and policies that will be made in our near future may disregard and not represent those for whom our gathering, caring, building, and sharing is ultimately meaningful. World-changing events often occur in circumstances and at times when we would never imagine their having the power to do what they do. Let us keep in mind that a tired women sitting down on a bus, without intending to do so, changed our lives and our world. By taking her own weariness more seriously than the laws and conventions that ignored it, she gave us good news and new life. It is in the ordinary parts of our lives, when we try simply to be the strongest, most human person we can become, and when we help each other do the same, that we will do the great things we have no way of foretelling. And for many there is and will increasingly be a need to rest their weary bones in the comfort, challenge, and support of our taking each other seriously.

5

Seeing through the Camouflage: Jonathan as Unconventional Nurturer

THE STORY WITHIN THE STORY

AS TOLD IN THE BIBLE, Samuel was the last of the judges to rule over all of ancient Israel. His anointing of Saul as its first king began a new kind of leadership for Israel. The Old Testament books of Samuel (1 and 2 Samuel) recount this transition from the period of judges to the period of kings. 1 Samuel tells of King Saul's reign, his failure and death. 2 Samuel tells of the subsequent rise and success of David as king. Jonathan was Saul's devoted son and David's closest friend.

    The story of Jonathan and David's relationship is scattered and weaves throughout 1 and 2 Samuel, a story among and within other stories.[1] I abridge and bring together the various parts of the story of Jonathan and David as follows:

> *Jonathan, the son of King Saul, was a brave and daring warrior; but his military exploits at Geba and Michmash did not effectively remove the threat posed by the Philistines. When Israel was desperate and suffering defeat, David, a young, inexperienced soldier and unlikely hero, intervened to slay the Philistines' champion, Goliath. The Philistines fled, and the men of Israel pursued and defeated them.*

Having seen David go forth against the Philistine, King Saul sent for him. And David was brought before him with the head of Goliath in his hand.

When David had finished speaking to Saul, the whole self of Jonathan was knit to the whole self of David, and Jonathan loved David as his own self. Saul took David into his own house. Then Jonathan made a covenant with David, because he loved him as his own self. And Jonathan stripped himself of the robe that was upon him and gave it to David, and also his armor, and even his sword and his bow and belt.

David went out and was successful wherever King Saul sent him. But the people began to praise David more than Saul, and this displeased Saul.

So Saul spoke to Jonathan and all his servants that they should kill David. But Jonathan delighted much in David and told him, "Saul my father seeks to kill you; therefore stay in a secret place and hide yourself; and if I learn anything, I will come and tell you."

Then Jonathan went to Saul and spoke well of David and recounted his service to Saul. And Saul hearkened to the voice of Jonathan.

But there was war again; and David went and made a great slaughter among the Philistines. Jealousy and anger returned to Saul. As he sat in his house with a spear in his hand, and David was playing the harp, Saul sought to pin him to the wall with the spear; but David eluded Saul, and he fled and escaped.

Saul's anger was also kindled against Jonathan. And Saul said to Jonathan, "You son of a perverse, rebellious woman, do I not know that you have chosen David to your own shame? Therefore, send and fetch him to me, for he shall surely die."

Then Jonathan answered Saul his father, "Why should David be put to death? What has he done?" But Saul cast his spear at Jonathan to smite him; so Jonathan knew that he was determined to put David to death.

Jonathan left in anger, and he ate no food for days because he worried about David, whom his father had disgraced. He went to be with David in their secret meeting place. When they met, they kissed one another and wept with one another, and David took great courage. Saying that God would always bind them, they pledged their lives to each other forever before they parted. Jonathan returned to the city.

But David, who had fled to the wilderness, was afraid because Saul sought to kill him. So Jonathan rose and went to David in the wilderness and strengthened him. And Jonathan said to David, "Fear not; for the hand of Saul my father shall not find you; you shall be king over Israel, and I shall be next to you." And the two of them made a covenant together again before Yahweh, the god of Israel; and David remained in the wilderness, and Jonathan went home.

But later on Jonathan and Saul were slain in battle against the Philistines. And when that news was brought to David, David took hold of his clothes and rent them, and he mourned and fasted, and, crying out for Jonathan, lamented:

> "Thy glory, O Israel, is slain upon
> thy high places!
> How are the mighty fallen!

> "Saul and Jonathan, beloved and lovely!
> In life and death they were not divided;
> they were swifter than eagles,
> they were stronger than lions.
> How are the mighty fallen
> in the midst of the battle!

> "Jonathan lies slain upon thy high places.
> I am distressed for you, my brother Jonathan;
> very pleasant have you been to me;
> your love to me was wonderful,
> passing the love of women.

> "How are the mighty fallen,
> and the weapons of war perished!"

In the contests for control among powerful men after Saul's death, David became king over Israel. He sent for Meribbaal, the crippled

son of Jonathan, and said to him, "Do not fear; for I will show you
kindness for the sake of your father Jonathan, and I will restore to
you all of Saul's land; and you shall eat at my table always."

During David's campaign to unite a divided land, Meribbaal's
servant came to him to say that Meribbaal had betrayed and deserted
David. The servant hoped to gain what his master owned. But on
returning to his house, David found Meribbaal waiting for him, re-
lieved that David had returned safely, and with no interest in Saul's
former holdings.

When the Gibeonites demanded the lives of seven of Saul's sons as
payment for the damage that Saul had once done to them, David
said, "I will give them"; but he spared Meribbaal because of the
covenant of Yahweh which was between David and Jonathan.

Afterwards, David went and took the bones of Saul and the bones
of Jonathan from the men who had stolen them from the public
square where the Philistines had hanged them on the day that they
had killed Saul and Jonathan in battle. And David brought up from
there the bones of Saul and the bones of Jonathan and buried them
in their native region of Benjamin. [2]

In the following sections I will fill in some details and elaborate on
the story of Jonathan and David, and attempt to interpret its meaning for today.

REBEL WARRIOR

The story begins with the image of Jonathan as an individu-
alistic and heroic warrior. He bravely strikes down the pillar of the
Philistines at Geba. Such pillars were erected to establish a ruler's
claims, and knocking over one would have been sufficient to in-
augurate a retaliatory war, which is what follows.[3] Jonathan's action
does not do concrete damage nor give Israel a military advantage;
instead it provokes a counterattack for which Israel is not prepared.

Jonathan's subsequent defense at Michmash is not much
greater. He targets a weakened post; his plan is sudden and not well
considered; his success depends to a large extent on his armor bearer;
together they kill only twenty. The ensuing battle in which the men

of Israel join is neither great nor conclusive. Jonathan as a warrior is impulsive and inspirational. The people like him and vociferously defend him when Saul scolds him for his risky military maneuvers. He is able to rally them and gain their support. But he cannot effectively lead them to victory.[4]

One scholar writes: "When I Samuel opens at the end of the period of the judges, Israel appears as a loose congeries of tribes . . . and capable from time to time under temporary leaders of common action, but powerless to resist the dominant power in Palestine. When II Samuel closes, the tribes have been welded into a powerful nation."[5] Jonathan is such a temporary military leader, a warrior who faces an ominous military obstacle against which he lacks the preparation and capability to fight, and who consequently recognizes David's qualifications to lead.

PERSON OF YAHWEH

Although Jonathan's military performance is not notable for leadership, body count, or strategic outcome, the directness of his relationship with Yahweh, the god of Israel, does stand out. While his father Saul performs cultic activities and consults priests before going into battle, Jonathan avoids the priests, approaches Yahweh directly, and rushes into battle.[6] He even speaks for Yahweh—"For Yahweh has given them into the hand of Israel."[7] Jonathan's battle is identical with Yahweh's battle and is in Yahweh's complete control. Not outcomes, but Yahweh's overriding influence, is central to Jonathan's story.[8] Jonathan (his name meaning "Yahweh has given") is victorious not because he has won a battle or led Israel, but, as the story says, "because he has been at work with God today."

This prominent and distinguishing characteristic of Jonathan as a person of Yahweh is well established in the story by the time he becomes the maker of a covenant with David.

COVENANT MAKER

In the ancient Near East covenants were agreements or oaths made to resolve differences between conflicting parties, vassal and lord, or conqueror and conquered.[9] The word *love* used in covenant making denoted the kind of attachment people had to a king more than interpersonal affection.[10] Such a covenant would read, for example, as "A vassal must love his sovereign. . . . 'You will love as yourselves Assurbanipal.'"[11]

Within the Bible, the God of Israel sometimes proposes and makes a covenant with his troubled, helpless, disobedient, or difficult children; and sometimes conflicts are settled and agreements made between various people in the form of a covenant.[12]

When Jonathan and David make their covenant, however, Yahweh is not a party nor do Jonathan and David have conflicts to resolve or obedience and superiority to establish. Scholars usually admit that "it is difficult to interpret the covenant between David and Jonathan," because there are "no stipulated obligations."[13]

Some assume that as King Saul's son, Jonathan is his "rightful successor," and that in the covenant he voluntarily waives his right and gives David the throne.[14] But in the narrative preceding this covenant, Samuel has already told Saul that he has failed as king, that his kingship has ended, and that Yahweh has "appointed" another man "to be prince over his people."[15] The task of and responsibility for choosing Israel's next king is not Jonathan's, and his involvement with David is not about royal acquiescence.

The usual English version—"Then Jonathan made a covenant with David"—favors Jonathan with initiation, but this is an interpretation and adaptation, not a literal translation, of the Hebrew text. Usually, covenant making is expressed as a sentence made up of a subject (the superior party), verb ("made"), direct object ("a covenant"), a preposition ("with"), and its object (the inferior party): "So-and-so made a covenant with so-and-so."[16] But in the Jonathan-David covenant the conjunction "and," instead of a preposition for "with," precedes David's name. The subject of the sentence appears to be "Jonathan and David," but the verb is singular. A literal transition would have to be something like "Jonathan and David, he made a covenant." Translators have typically resolved the inconsistency of the Hebrew sentence by assuming that the conjunction "and" was meant to be the preposition "with."

I would suggest, however, that because conventional covenant making served the superior-inferior relationship of parties brought into an agreement, the usual formula and terms did not suit the nature of Jonathan and David's relationship and had to be modified, even if somewhat awkwardly.[17] Indeed, one scholar notes that "friendship of this sort was a rare thing between equals of different family backgrounds."[18]

The equality and mutuality of Jonathan and David's relationship are reinforced and formalized later in their story when "the two of them" renew their covenant in the wilderness (this time with plural subject and plural verb firmly in place).[19]

JONATHAN'S LOVE, YAHWEH'S ACTION

Throughout the rest of the story, after Jonathan and David's initial covenant making, their covenant is referred to as "of" or "before" Yahweh, but never as made or controlled by Yahweh. Yahweh is present in but not maker of the covenant. Instead, Jonathan speaks to David with Yahweh's authority when he reassures him after Saul threatens David's life; he goes to David in the wilderness to "strengthen his hand in God"; and the two of them make their "covenant before Yahweh." The "kindness for Jonathan's sake" that David wishes to show to the survivors of Saul's house is expressed soon after as "the kindness of God."[20]

Jonathan and David's covenant is not the product or result of obedience to God; rather, God is present in the midst of their relationship: "Yahweh shall be between me and you . . . for ever."[21] Jonathan's love is Yahweh's action, not the outcome of Yahweh's directions and permission.

Yahweh—not as authority, but as love—is basic to this covenant. To Saul, pious and concerned for his own position, it makes no sense. He interprets it as perversity, rebellion, preference for companionship that is antifamilial. Saul sees David and Jonathan's relationship as "a league . . . against me," and misses again, as he did as the pious observer of priestly ritual before war, his son's direct experience of and relationship with Yahweh.[22]

In the context of vying for territory and control, Jonathan and David's covenant does not make sense politically. They do not fight each other's military battles; Jonathan actually stays with and fights alongside of Saul, and David deliberately avoids and does not attack Saul. They conspire to love each other and keep each other safe; they do not conspire to gain power or to overthrow Saul. They aid each other in providing not material support or political gain, but nurture and comfort. They are there for each other at the most difficult times—when their safety is threatened and when they are frightened, worried, or lonely.

THE CHARACTER OF JONATHAN

Jonathan is an unusual character, and biblical scholars have had difficulty accepting him. They have assigned labels and characteristics to him that he does not warrant, and they have overlooked those qualities that make him unique. He is dismissed for his "naivete and simplistic view of good and evil"[23] and described as "not normal, flat, static, certainly opaque"; his "attitudes and actions [are said to lack] any normal motivation."[24] Scholars for the most part have been uncomfortable with Jonathan, and they refuse or are unable to recognize him as the interesting and complex character he is, one who is unconventional, pushy, and aggressive as well as gentle, calm, and nurturing. It is this latter image of Jonathan as lover or nurturer that nudges readers to accept uncomfortably a man with motives other than material and political success, a man who stands by his man for love, not gain.

Jonathan affects David and Saul, but he is never the force that gives either one the edge or advantage over the other. Within the highly competitive and conflictual relationships throughout 1 and 2 Samuel, Jonathan's love for and relationship with David is present and insistent, but it is not causal. Jonathan is a nurturer, not a main player. Against the scheming, deception, and contests throughout 1 and 2 Samuel, Jonathan establishes an intimate, nurturing, vulnerable relationship that promises no political gain.

The body of scholarship that interprets Jonathan and David's covenant as Jonathan's abdication to David's kingship may be an attempt to rationalize the disbelief and annoyance that many may feel, but cannot reasonably explain, when confronted by noncompetitive, intimate, loving relationships between men. Gay men, especially those who have risked coming out in some or all aspects of their lives, more readily recognize and credit human love and not politics as the arena of David and Jonathan's relationship; and we do not flinch when Jonathan risks social security and familial approval for personal affection.

CAMOUFLAGED LOVER?

But why must the Jonathan-David relationship be set in the context of a covenant? If Jonathan and David were not political rivals in need of resolving problems, why the covenant form? The covenant may have been a convenient form for saying something that could not be said another way. Some observations about literary form and theme may help to further our understanding of the use of covenant.

Joseph Cady in his work on Walt Whitman states that gay writers writing in a time that is hostile to gay people had to invent protective strategies that would allow them to express themselves while sufficiently guarding themselves against social exposure and punishment.[25]

Cady goes on to say that gay writers in nineteenth-century America and Great Britain made imaginative expropriations from existing popular frameworks, adapting terms that they felt were also applicable to or potentially true about the homosexual bond. Such a term for Walt Whitman was *adhesion*, which he borrowed from a popular movement during his time known as phrenology. Other terms involved the language of friendship and comradeship.[26] If the situation for gay writers during biblical times was similar, such appropriate terms might have been conventional to covenant making. The altering and coding of terms would have been heard by other gay men with a recognizing ear.[27]

Cady states further that a common convention in nineteenth-century male homosexual literature was the elegy, which was an effective cover permitting intense and open expression of love, because the praised one was, after all, dead. Another convention was soldier comradeship, even less discernible than ordinary comradeship since men were together not by preference and the absence of women required their tending to one another.[28]

Such invention could have occurred in the 1 and 2 Samuel narrative. I am not saying that the particular inventions of nineteenth-century American homosexual writers would have been the same as those of the writers in biblical times. In each period, writers would make use of what was available and code it accordingly. But David's lament for Jonathan fits the elegy and soldier comrade vehicles too perfectly not at least to mention. As an accepted literary convention, the lament or elegy would not have aroused suspicion. The sharing of attention between Saul and Jonathan provides a good cover (how many have pointed out that David owed none of those comments to Saul?), and terms like *beloved and lovely*, *love*, and *brother* have erotic as well as safe fraternal associations.[29] The introduction of Jonathan's son later in the narrative would provide the ultimate cover.

FELLOW LOVER

The conventional and socially acceptable language and form of covenant, friendship, politics, elegy, and soldiering may have been used to tell a love story that needed both to remain within what was socially acceptable as well as to break with convention, that is, to tell a story that would appeal to and be heard differently by two different audiences.

I have read the arguments for whether or not homosexuality was practiced at the time of and specifically by Jonathan and David. The argument that most cultures in the ancient Near East allowed homosexual practices is not convincing to me because the counterargument can always be made that basic to Israel was Yahweh's admonition to be unlike its neighbors. At any rate, I do not doubt that homosexuality was not socially accepted during most of biblical times. I do assume, however, that some people desired same-gender affection and sexual contact, and I am interested in their efforts to express themselves. It is less important to me that David and Jonathan might have had a homosexual relationship than that a writer or writers may have used an available framework to tell a story that would be read or heard differently by gay men than by nongay people.[30]

Gay men today, then, may embrace Jonathan as a fellow lover because of those who wrote, compiled, and edited his story. We identify with Jonathan because of what the writers of his story were able to tell us. We find strength for ourselves because the story is about and by others who have lived through and coped with problems similar to our own and who endeavored to express themselves as we do. We grasp support for our own struggle from the survival of Jonathan's story and how it came to be told.

Against the objections of his father, but with the blessing of his God and his feelings of affection, Jonathan builds and sustains a loving relationship with David. Within 1 and 2 Samuel the Jonathan story engages the larger narrative to point to needed social changes in military, political, and religious organization. The Jonathan who emerges in this story and in the larger narrative is unconventional in love, in war, as a son, as a man. Within the social context within which Jonathan's story was compiled and written, I would suggest that gay writers were able to include his story as a message and signal to others who seek an alternative to business as usual.[31]

I shall close by drawing a parallel between the song of Hannah, which begins 1 Samuel, and David's elegy, which begins 2 Samuel.

Hannah was the mother of Samuel, the judge who anointed Saul as Israel's first king. The theme of her song is captured in these verses:
The bows of the mighty are broken,
but the feeble gird on strength.
. . . for not by might shall a man prevail. (1 Sam. 2:4, 9c)[32]

So, also, in David's elegy, "How the mighty are fallen!" is repeated three times, once followed by "in the midst of battle" and another time by "and the weapons of war perished." In between these two songs, Saul reigns and falls, the initiator and victim of war by the mighty. And David is not immune to involvement in these contests for power that were reshaping Israel.

If in his lament David does indeed see that might has not prevailed and that the weapons of war are destroyed, must he not also recognize that Jonathan's allegiance to Saul, his returning again and again to fight by his side, has indeed been at the expense of Jonathan and David's love for each other? Might not a more humane, or more divine, choice, one with more enduring and sustaining consequences, have been for Jonathan not to return home, for David not to have let him go, for both of them to have dared to build a life together which was not yet? In spite of the social conditions that made such a choice "unrealistic" or "impossible," is not the power of the story that we yearn for a different ending and want to make it happen in our own lives? Does not the sadness we feel at Jonathan and David's loss of each other remind us to build our lives and families around our affective needs instead of conforming and sacrificing them to social convention, to tend to our personal relationships and find God in our caring for and nurturing one another, rather than in the idols of material gain and might?

6

Leaving Jesus:
A Theology of Friendship and Autonomy

AFFILIATED WITH PERSECUTION?

SOMETIME AGO I read an interview with a member of a gay Nazi organization. The interviewer asked whether belonging to such an organization was not a contradiction, since Nazis persecuted gays. The man responded that it was not any more of a contradiction than identifying as a gay Christian.

For those of us who are uncomfortable with many parts, if not the whole direction of, Christian tradition and history, such a comment may spark a moment of defense, apology, denial, admission, or confession. Probably one would be hard pressed to find any tradition that is free of persecutions and oppression; but that does not make the Christian church's record of having endorsed, initiated, or participated in brutal exercises of power any easier for us to take or rationalize. We know that the church has been slow to respond to the cries of the oppressed and has often sided with or been the oppressor.[1]

Those of us who do not want to apologize for or cover up the church's practice often feel cornered, having to defend an oppressive

91

institution. How many of us have friends, colleagues, and family members who ask us why we remain involved with an institution that is as likely to ignore or abuse people as it is to welcome and include them? We deserve their questions and we owe them explanations.

Lapsed from Humble Origins?

One way that we justify remaining within the church is to see it as lapsed—lapsed from its primitive roots, its egalitarian and communitarian origins before the Roman Emperor Constantine accommodated, co-opted, and brought it within the hierarchical ordering of state power. Although we may agree with the gay Nazi that to be a gay Christian—or a liberal, revolutionary, female, African American, poor, or peace-and-justice-making Christian— appears to be something of a contradiction, we are probably quick to point out that whereas fascism is based on exclusion, supremacy, and brutal enforcement, Christianity is not. The church has simply gone astray from a basis, center, origin in a common carpenter who welcomed, included, and healed the broken, outcast, and needy. But Christians do have this model, this example, against which to evaluate and correct our practice. Fascism does not. The church has an intention, purpose, and rootedness, which however much obscured and ignored, can be resurrected, held up, returned to.

Those of us who find ourselves mostly at odds with and on the margins of the institutional and larger church often appeal to this basis; and we feel compelled to defend our actions as consistent with the example of Jesus. We may say we organize, march, demonstrate, resist, and protest because that is what Jesus did or would have done. We stand with the poor because Jesus stood with the poor. We support equal rights for women, lesbians, gay men, and people of color because that is what Jesus would do if he were here. Jesus would have been on our side. Jesus was about changing the world as we are changing it. And the church would do well to correct itself and see that.

Perhaps we are right. It is what I often say. But I think we need to stop using Jesus as our trump card in waging the struggle for peace and justice. First, because it is opportunistic; we use him as we wish for our own ends. Second, because we really do not mean it; I do not think we are involved in movements for social change because Jesus would have been with us, but because *we* want, need, and think we ought to be involved. Jesus gets tagged on as a rationale or support for what we know or have decided we should do. And third, because it is not an effective strategy; the organized, mainstream church has more power for establishing the prevailing image of Jesus than do marginalized people within or outside it. The history of Christianity has shown that Jesus is up for grabs; and whoever is most powerful determines the prevailing image of Jesus.

Preferred, Competing, Prevailing Images

We know quite well by now that there is no single Jesus or one coherent Jesus story in the Bible. There are four stories, four gospels. And each varies, has a different emphasis, was intended for and addressed to a different audience. Matthew's Jesus is the upholder of Jewish law; Mark's Jesus is the healer; Luke's is the compassionate friend of the lowly; and John's Jesus embodies contemporary philosophical concepts.

It would be an incredible, and probably impossible, feat to roll these stories into one and come up with the definitive Jesus. The variation in the ways the stories are told and the diversity of actions and characteristics do not yield easily to a smooth, even-edged fabric. So, like the different storytellers themselves and the communities for whom the stories were told, we continue to pick and choose what we need Jesus to be for us. We select and embellish those parts of the stories that complement our own stories and satisfy our own needs. We ignore or play down the rest. And one can, if one wants, construct from the stories images of Jesus that range from a mighty warrior with a sword,[2] to a heavenly king,[3] a homeless man without a place to rest his head,[4] an angry and nasty social critic,[5] or a personal friend who walks with us, talks with us, and tells us we are his own.[6]

You may be saying, "Yes, but within the gospels some images are more prevalent than others; there is after all an underlying characteristic or mode of behavior that overarches the others." And I would say that we are feeling the strength of our bias, however just and necessary it may be in today's movements for social change. For we perhaps too conveniently emphasize the Jesus who favors the lowly, but overlook his favoring, as well, tax collectors,[7] rulers,[8] an official,[9] and a Roman centurion who tells him "I am a man . . . with soldiers under me; and I say to one, 'Go,' and he goes, and to another, 'Come,' and he comes, and to my slave, 'Do this,' and he does it."[10] Or perhaps we brush past that moment when Jesus advises easing up on giving to the poor for the sake of extravagant gift giving and special caring between two people.[11]

> Now when Jesus was at Bethany in the house of Simon the leper, a woman came up to him with an alabaster flask of very expensive ointment, and she poured it on his head, as he sat at table. But when the disciples saw it, they were indignant, saying, "Why this waste? For this ointment might have been sold for a large sum, and given to the poor." But Jesus, aware of this, said to them, "Why do you trouble the woman? For she has done a beautiful thing to me. For you always have the poor with you, but you will not always have me."[12]

From the various and rich imagery within the New Testament, I too prefer the image of Jesus as the inclusive, human, lowly one; and our sharing that image is one of the reasons that many of us work and gather together. But others gathered elsewhere are as firmly invested in the primary characteristic and image that *they* have identified. They are, for example, as convinced that Jesus would have told lesbian/gay people what he told the adulterous woman—to "go and sin no more"[13]—as we are that he would have welcomed such people just as they are.

For those of us who need to persuade, convince, and win—and in the social justice movement the need to do so seems great—

acknowledging that the four stories about Jesus lend themselves to a variety of images and interpretations may not be easy to accept. That the Bible is a resource for defining and lending strength to the formation of various faith communities that believe and act in various, and often conflicting, ways is not easy for those whose faith community is predicated on being right and changing others. To acknowledge and allow for a multiplicity of expressions may be to tolerate forms of Christianity that are unacceptably oppressive. But to argue for the primacy of one form, our form, over another is to become engaged in a contest for which there is no winner. Each community can claim a biblically based Jesus who supports it. On and on we go, insisting that we have the right interpretation and apologizing for or criticizing those who have interpreted incorrectly and killed in the name of Jesus Christ.

The plethora of Christian denominations and sects attests to this ongoing conflict and separation. Within each a particular image of Jesus is affirmed or emphasized. If one does not agree with the proffered image, one is better off finding a denomination whose image is more suitable. Perhaps the image that unites or is most common to many denominations is that of "Jesus Christ as Lord and Savior." The image of Jesus as Lord is a strong and commanding one. When I have challenged it as authoritarian and dictatorial, I have been quickly reminded of the paradox built into it.[14] The rejoinder goes something like, "Yes, but, the one we call Lord is not a wealthy, ruthless, powerful king, but a humble, helpful carpenter; we are talking about the rule of humility, not about establishing a despot." But that is exactly what they are doing with Jesus. We establish the image that we think is right, the leader that we can follow, the example, no matter how lowly and humble, that is the supreme and commanding one for our lives. If we cannot convince others to join us or believe in that image, they can go somewhere else. And whether we say it loudly or not, we think they are following their own fabricated version of Jesus.

This arrangement may sound a bit like the pluralistic ideal of various faith communities coexisting, each determining its own beliefs and practices. But within our social order, those with the most power get to claim, name, interpret, and establish the dominant image of Jesus. So it should not surprise us that the image of Jesus that prevails within and is made socially normative by the circles of powers, the mainstream denominations, is not first and foremost a scruffy kickabout with radical politics and a commitment to upsetting the applecart, but a lord, a master, one who is in control, who controls, who rules—an image identical with those who prefer and have the power to establish that image.

The Flattening Effect of Images

Even when the prevailing image is of one who suffered extreme degradation and physical agony, it takes on the triumphalist and superlative quality of leveling or ignoring the particular and ordinary suffering of others, of those in our midst, of ourselves, for no one's suffering is or was as great as Jesus'.

In a 1954 interview with François Mauriac, "the illustrious Catholic member of the [French] Acadámie," Elie Wiesel recalls listening to "an impassioned, fascinating monologue" on "the greatness and divinity of the Jew Jesus." "Every reference led back to him." After a while, "something in [Mauriac's] discourse irritated [Wiesel] so much that for the first time in [his] life [he] exhibited bad manners" and gave "in to an angry impulse":

> *"Sir," I said, "you speak of Christ. Christians love to speak of him. The passion of Christ, the agony of Christ, the death of Christ. In your religion, that is all you speak of. Well, I want you to know that ten years ago, not very far from here, I knew Jewish children every one of whom suffered a thousand times more, six million times more, than Christ on the cross. And we don't speak about them. Can you understand that, sir? We don't speak about them."*

Mauriac's response, however, was not defensive, and it may serve to show us a way out of a tradition of triumphalist theology. He was visibly humbled, he wept, "he bade [Wiesel to] continue speaking," he "questioned." Instead of attempting to clarify or defend what he had said or meant about *Jesus*, Mauriac "wanted to know everything," all of the "details," about *Wiesel's* experience in the Nazi death camps. He encouraged him to "speak out," to break his vow about never writing about "those events." A year later Wiesel would send Mauriac the manuscript of *Night*, his first book about his experiences in the camps.[15]

The problem for Christians is not simply one of who images Jesus as what. The problem is in imaging Jesus at all—in trying to claim him as who he really was and as who he really is for us. For such efforts can only catch us up in heroicizing and glorifying a single individual at the expense of the particular experiences and lives of the many in our midst—the very lives that Jesus himself attended to in his own time.

THE LIMITATIONS OF THE MASTER'S TOOLS

Even if we want to take on the established powers by challenging the prevailing image, by asserting what we consider to be the correct interpretation of Jesus, by replacing it with our own preferred image, Jesus would still remain a lord, master, king. For within Christianity, within the church, within groups on the church's periphery, to image Jesus "correctly" is to engage is making Jesus superlative; and no matter in which way Jesus is understood or imaged as superlative, he remains the head, the boss, the chief, the master. If we could somehow make him definitively the master of liberation, the king of the poor, the supreme example of the struggle for justice, he would remain first and foremost master, king, and perfect example of whatever it is that we see as most important. We would at most replace one lord with another. For once we begin to argue, work, or live exclusively for our preferred image of Jesus, we either strengthen the definition of that image or alter it in such a way that it remains more securely *the* image.

Within a church that is hierarchically organized, imaging Jesus will inevitably result in a powerful man who knows what he is doing, knows what is best for the church, and can tell us what is best to do. Our own efforts to defend or reform the church or to defend it as lapsed from its roots confirm this tendency to look for solutions in a masterly figure, for we typically propose an image of Jesus who will set the church right. We accept the ground rules for debate and power making within the church. To argue convincingly and to be heard within the context of the church, we inevitably accede to its terms and its language.

When proposing changes or opposing church policy and faced with the reality of our being defeated or not heard, we feel pressed to say sooner or later and somewhat desperately, "But Jesus would not have done it that way." We yield to talking in terms of who has and is authority, because that is the language that is listened to and understood; and then our proposals are incorporated into the prevailing image or dismissed because what Jesus would have done has already been decided and agreed upon.

In Audre Lorde's terms: "The master's tools will never dismantle the master's house. They may allow us temporarily to beat him at his own game, but they will never enable us to bring about genuine change." We may gain the occasional acknowledgment that there is some truth to our image of Jesus. But those accommodations "will never enable us to bring about genuine change."[16] To be occupied with arguing over the correct image of Jesus is to be caught up in establishing and recognizing him as a master. Over and over we end up with a "top man" in whom we put our hope and trust, instead of giving ourselves and each other the power to decide and do what should be done, instead of taking responsibility for claiming and doing it ourselves.

Friend, Not Master

Jesus, according to the Gospel of John, seemed to have understood the pitfall of following a master and wanted no part of being one:

> You call me Teacher and Lord; and you are right, for so I am. If I then, your Lord and Teacher, have washed your feet, you also ought to wash one another's feet. For I have given you an example, that you also should do as I have done. Truly, truly, I say to you, slaves are not greater than their master.
>
> But no longer do I call you slaves, for slaves do not know what their master is doing. Now I call you friends, for all that I have heard from my God I have made known to you.

*I am with you only a little while longer; and you will want to seek
me, but where I am going you cannot come. So a new commandment I give to you, that you love one another. As I have loved you,
you also should love one another. By this all people will know that
you are my disciples, if you have love for one another.*[17]

Those of us who still define the master's house as their only source
of support, those who still insist on establishing and hearkening to
the correct example of Jesus, the Jesus we should follow, do not do
it because the master requires or suggests that we do it. Our making
Jesus the master or authoritative example does not seem to have
been his idea. And he does not seem to have wanted to found an
organization that would be preoccupied with fawning over him and
perfecting his image.

Quite remarkably, it is Jesus as the master who says, "Don't look
to me for answers; you're on your own. If you want my advice, and
it's last I'm going to give you, it's that you work things out with each
other. Look to each other; don't look to me. I'm not the boss, simply
a friend who's soon dead and gone. Good-bye." A friend bids us well,
not holding on to us with last-minute conditions about loyalty and
preserving his name, but trusting and expecting us to love one
another—a rare and wonderful example of rescinding patriarchal
privilege, and perhaps one that many would do well to follow. But
its value and power lie not in proposing yet another example of how
wonderful Jesus is, but settles on us the task of being our own
example, of finding out from each other how wonderful we can be
for each other. The example does not offer up yet another master;
it shatters the master-slave relationship into one of friendship, and
not a sentimental friendship of holding on and dependence, but a
friendship of challenge, letting go, and affirming independence.

My reading of Scripture and my image here is selective; and I
may seem as guilty as those whom I accuse of tailoring their images
of Jesus. But I think I lift up that which does not get said so frequently
because it threatens to replace the master's tools, and then, of
course, the master's house. Where would the church be as we know
it if Jesus were not central and on top? But I readily concede that

my reading of Scripture and my imaging is selective and partial; however, and more important, the point I am making can be done without reading Scripture or without imaging Jesus. For I know, and I have learned, that we need to love one another, not because I was raised a Christian, not because I have read the Bible, and not because Jesus is my savior.

Finding Others to Love

I know that we need to love one another because of my needs and my despair and because of those who respond to them. Those who have responded to my needs most readily and welcomed me most unequivocally have been outside of or on the margins of the church. They were not folks guided by the church to help me. And I cannot help seeing that the mainstream church is not typically in the forefront of waging struggles for freedom.[18]

In the early years of the civil rights movement, Martin Luther King, Jr.'s "Letter from Birmingham Jail" captured the reluctance of his "fellow clergymen" and the "church as a whole" to "meet the challenge" of the "decisive hour" and "come to the aid of justice."[19] The church was and is late also to recognize and advance the women's movement; and it is resistant and hostile still to welcoming lesbians and gay men.

Those who gather in the name of Jesus do not seem prepared to respond to emerging cries for help and recognition. This is not an observation that only I have made, nor has it been made only recently. In 1924, as a pastor in Detroit, Reinhold Niebuhr lamented:

> The church has lost the chance to become the unifying element in our American society. It is not anticipating new facts. It is merely catching up slowly to the new social facts created by economic and other forces. . . .
>
> What we accomplish in the way of church unity ought to be accepted with humility and not hailed with pride. We are not creating. We are merely catching up with creation.[20]

Those who are not beholding to Jesus and not affiliated with the Christian church are more often the ones who are ready and at the forefront of responding to human needs. They do not seem to need Jesus to make them that way, whereas those who rely on Jesus take a long time getting there and often never do.

My own current participation in the church is predicated on having left it, on finding welcome and nurture in the nonchurched lesbian/gay community, and then on returning, strengthened and confident as a gay man, to try to make a place for myself and other lesbian/gay/bisexual people within it. My reliable source of support for doing this remains lesbians and gay men outside of the church; and I often find myself retreating to them to rest and renew my strength for the battles and homophobia that rage and fester within the church. I wish the church were the place where I could rest, be whole, and work, but it is not.

A Changing, Bumpy Road

So what does this mean for the affiliation that some of us have with the Christian church and tradition? We need to ask where we stand with the church, with Jesus Christ, and with Christianity.

As regards the established church, we often need and are not afraid to stand outside it; with Audre Lorde we "stand outside the circle of this society's definition of [acceptability]"; our identities are "forged in the crucibles of difference" as we learn "how to make common cause with those others identified as outside the structures in order to define and seek a world in which we can all flourish."[21] Two national surveys that I conducted of lesbian/gay/bisexual people in the United Church of Christ and the United Methodist church show that standing on the outside, working on human needs, and bringing people together tend to be our common practice. Three-quarters of both lay and clergy respondents report active involvement in ministry outside of their respective denominations, most often in the form of AIDS advocacy and services, volunteer counseling, lesbian/gay support services and activism, hunger and homeless projects, community services, social justice advocacy, interfaith events and organizations, women's antiviolence projects, and youth programs.[22]

As regards Jesus, we remember him as a friend, as a friend who has departed, and who in his own terms said, I am dead, you are alive. Jesus gives us not a model to follow, not a how-to for running our lives, but a nudge to get on without him—to carry on our own lives as our own persons interacting with other persons in our own Galilees, in our own mixture of problems, people, joys, relationships. It is a nudging into who we are and what we need now, into getting on with what needs to be done, into loving one another. The resurrection is not some tricky maneuver of raising the actual body of Christ or even of devotedly remembering everything he was and said we should do; the resurrection is instead lifting up our own lives, taking responsibility for making them full and responsive to the lives around us.

And as regards Christianity, I turn to Buddhist poet Gary Snyder for some advice. In his collection of poems and essays titled *Turtle Island*, "the old/new name for the continent," Snyder writes about an American Indian understanding of personal autonomy and its potential for building community:

> *Each living being is a swirl in the flow, a formal turbulence, a "song." The land, the planet itself, is also a living being—at another pace. Anglos, Black people, Chicanos, and others beached up on these shores all share such views at the deepest levels of their cultural traditions—African, Asian, or European. Hark again to those roots, to see our ancient solidarity, and then to the work of living together on Turtle Island.*[23]

Hark to our roots and then to the work of living together. Perhaps, we see or find our roots in those wandering folks, our biblical ancestors, told of in the Book of Genesis:

> *And Yahweh said to Abraham and Sarah, "Go from your country and from your kin and from your parents' house to the land that I will show you. And I will make of you a great nation; and I will bless you; and by you all the families of the earth shall bless themselves."*

So Sarah and Abraham went, as Yahweh had told them. They went to the land of Canaan, but it was occupied. So they went on to the desert, but there was great famine there. So then Abraham and Sarah went down to Egypt.[24]

With them we trace a journey through unknown lands, daring to cross boundaries and to build bridges into unfamiliar territories, but without invading, conquering, overpowering them. We seek to live among—not over or below—others; and we prepare ourselves for being turned away and welcomed, for retreating and insisting, for learning from others and contributing to them. Again and again, we pause to get our bearings yet another time on this bumpy road we call faith. Our roots are on the shifting, bumpy road traveled by Sarah and Abraham, thinking they were going one place and having to decide to go to another.

Ours is a tradition of difficult decisions without the promise of permanence, without the security of making the right decision once and forever. It is also the tradition of having a friend whom we do not own and who does not own us, does not beckon us, but trusts us to be on our own. Our tradition is one in which we beckon one another, softly and tenderly, or impatiently and earnestly, to get on with the work of loving one another, of living together. In hearkening to these roots we are propelled immediately into this time, this place, and the ongoing task of making ends meet, of living together on Turtle Island, of loving one another. We find this tradition updated and rehearsed with those and by those who live, work, and love between despair and rescue. We find it restated in the words of George Jackson, an imprisoned African-American man: "Settle your quarrels, come together, understand the reality of the situation, understand that fascism is already here. That people are already dying who could be saved, that generations more will die or live poor butchered half-lives if you fail to act. Do what must be done, discover your humanity and your love in revolution."[25]

7

Salvation:
Embodying Our Deepest Knowledge

Accepting the Nudge

In the previous chapter I spoke of the nudge that Jesus gives us to be on our own, to love one another. Here I accept that nudge to find and be found by others, to take responsibility for my life, and to respond to the lives of others. I try to discover what is most important or meaningful for me, to know what I am most enthused and concerned about. *Enthused* is derived from the ancient Greek *en theos*, meaning "in God" or "having God within"; and theologian Paul Tillich says one's "ultimate concern" is one's God.[1] That which is most important to us is our God; and our lives are most godlike when we embrace, take seriously, and share with others what is most important to us. I shall try to describe what ultimately concerns me, where and how I find God and God finds me, where and how my life becomes most meaningful.

To do this, I use the customary resources for theological reflection and formation—personal experience, Scripture, and tradition; and I shall also discuss and describe salvific or saving events. Scripture is literature that is considered sacred or special because it has a vital function, purpose, or application in our lives. Tradition is the handing over of advice, customs, and practices that are necessary for surviving and living in the present. Experience is our personal observations and encounters, and the knowledge, feelings, and changes that result from them. A salvific event is one that rescues us from pain and suffering and makes us a new person or people; it is an event that happens to us, rather than one that we make happen. I shall define each of these concepts a bit more extensively before applying them directly to myself.

Saving Events

Religion differs from philosophy in recognizing that we cannot always save ourselves and need to be saved by others. Philosophy is born of a confidence that one can stand back from or rise above one's situation, study it objectively, and resolve one's problems with reason. Religion recognizes that often an unexpected, ordinary encounter or experience rescues us from despair and gives us what we otherwise could not see or do by ourselves. To be sure, we are both philosophical and religious in our lives—we take the initiative and pull ourselves together as much as we need others to put us together; we think on our own, and we are taken care of.

The deliverance of slaves out of Egypt and the ministry of Jesus are events in which people are rescued, taken care of. The slaves cannot deliver themselves from their oppression. Yahweh needs to rescue them and sends the unlikely, reluctant, speech-impaired Moses to lead them. In spite of their expressed misery, the slaves are not ready and have to be jolted into action. Similarly, Jesus saves those who are outcast, alienated, and desperate; he is not the expected hero, but a common carpenter; and most are surprised by or do not believe in his ability.

Both rescue events address profound need and come in unexpected form. Both also crystalize in the ordinary, unnoticed arenas of human life: the complaints of a ragtag band of slaves and the events of everyday life on the streets of Galilee. Although the leading powers of the day are reported to have noticed, been annoyed by, and quickly dismissed these efforts, the events are played out in what is usually thought of as the insignificant levels of society. Neither are thoroughly or convincingly documented in history books.

The religious dimension of human life may seem dependent and passive, especially when compared with the take-charge, rational confidence of philosophy. And, indeed, there is about religion the acknowledgment that important things do happen for us, to us, and change us, whether we like it or not. Salvific events present themselves or impose themselves on us in ways that cannot easily be ignored.

But these events are summoned, determined, and shaped by our deepest needs. They are responses to the cries of oppression. Yahweh says, "I have seen the affliction of my people who are in Egypt" (Exod. 3:7); and Jesus says he comes "to set at liberty those who are oppressed" (Luke 4:18, 21). We are not forced to accept these events as much as we are compelled by the accuracy with which they address our needs. To refuse freedom is absurd, but to embrace it and change our lives completely is frightening as well. A significant part of the Exodus story has to do with resisting freedom and wanting to return to Egypt (Exod. 15:22-16:8); and in the Gospel of John, Jesus pointedly asks a sick man, "Do you want to be healed?" (John 5:6). The familiarity of despair to which we have become accustomed often complicates deciding for and accepting rescue/salvation.

The nonpassive, active, and necessary aspect of religion is our response to these saving events. We have the option simply to accept or reject them, and, if accepted, to decide, act, extend, and develop according to the opportunities they provide. They are saving events only if we respond to them by using the new freedom, autonomy, or empowerment to change our lives and make them more meaningful.

Instead of focusing solely on the Exodus and Jesus events, the two normative saving events of Christianity, I shall use their characteristics to identify current and personal saving events in my own life. Theologians Paul Tillich and Rudolf Bultmann share the view that the Christ event is authoritative not only within the Bible but because it occasions contemporary saving events.[2] I seek to recognize the unexpected, ordinary encounters with and actions by people that have saved and changed me.

SCRIPTURE

I skirt established Christian Scripture and tradition to gain autonomy, to locate myself within my own life, to escape an external authority and find an internal authority, to respond to my own need for the company of others. This is an act of independence, not of rebellion. My effort here is to push out, to name and claim what is important to me, not to discredit what has been named for, given to, or forced upon me.

Actually, the Bible encourages me to enlarge my recognition and appreciation of special stories outside of it; as a document compiled of writings from a variety of times, places, and experiences, it seems to be not so much a closed book as one that pushes at its own seams. Furthermore, my criterion for deciding what makes a story sacred is the same as that which Bultmann says makes the New Testament sacred for a Christian. According to David Kelsey, Bultmann claims:

> The faithful [person's] way of being-in-the-world is determined by the gospel's word of personal address in which he [or she] encounters a love accepting him [or her] for what he [or she] is. Living as one who understands [one]self that way, [one] is freed of the compulsion to assert [one]self against [one's] neighbor in order to coerce acknowledgement from him [or her]. Hence [one] is free to discern and meet the unique needs of [one's] neighbor. [One] sees [one's] whole world in a new way, as "gift." . . . This new creation is a present reality, and yet is ever future for it has to be realized anew again and again in repeated decisions to acknowledge [one]self acknowledged by God."[3]

I have begun to assemble and name as my Scripture a small body of literature in which I find myself accepted for who I am. I find this kind of acceptance and connection within E. M. Forster's *Maurice*, Hermann Hesse's *Siddhartha*, Toni Morrison's *Sula*, Audre Lorde's *Sister Outsider*, and Beth Brant's *Mohawk Trail*.[4]

I shall say more about *Maurice* later, and now shall only briefly say why I feel brought into and accepted within the other works. In *Siddhartha* an unexpected, ordinary person rescues another because "he knew how to listen": "He did not await anything with impatience and gave neither praise nor blame—he only listened. Siddhartha felt how wonderful it was to have such a listener who could be absorbed in another person's life, his strivings, his sorrows."[5] *Sula* describes a neighborhood of African-American people called the Bottom, in which, "aberrations were as much a part of nature as grace. . . . There was no creature so ungodly as to make them destroy it. They could kill easily if provoked to anger, but not by design, which explained why they could not 'mob kill' anyone. To do so was not only unnatural, it was undignified."[6] In *Sister Outsider* I am invited to reveal myself "in work and struggle together with those whom we define as different from ourselves," to create "patterns for relating across our human differences as equals"; we "do not have to become like each other in order to work together for a future [we] will all share."[7] In *Mohawk Trail* working-class people tell their stories and impart wisdom through a Native American woman: "Now, work is work, and if you're working and doin' what you're supposed to, you ain't got time for that name calling and prejudice stuff. . . . I say, if you work with a person long enough, you're just a plain fool if you can't see you're in it together. . . . You got to stick to each other. It's like bein' family. Lord knows, families can be a pain in the you-know-what, but nothin' ain't easy."[8]

These personal addresses and stories have the power to change how I relate to others, because having felt in them what it is like to be accepted, to belong, to be involved, I not only have a vision of how I want to live with others, I am not satisfied with anything short of it. As one who feels and understands myself as accepted, I can no longer beg, plead, or ask for permission from others. I see the world in a new way. I do not seek to coerce acknowledgment from others but to inform, interact, and contribute to others. These stories are not, of course, the world. They give me a feeling of what might or should be, but they themselves do not change the world; instead, they are a resource that builds expectations and shows me a new way to live in and change the world.

TRADITION

Instead of fumbling with my inherited tradition, with what has so overtly been handed over to me, I take what feels to me to be a more graceful and relaxed approach. Instead of accepting the oddness of not fitting into and not finding help in the practices and advice handed over to me, I try to step into familiarity and comfort. Instead of spending so much time rejecting and fighting with what seems expected of or forced on me, I seek to rest, to be soothed and reassured, to be challenged kindly. I need and look for solace and succor.

This "new" tradition, my acquired tradition, however, is not ready for the taking. It has not been formalized, recognized, put together for me. With other lesbians and gay men, I seek out and discover those who lived in ways that help me survive and live more fully today. We look to and examine the lives, messages, and activities of such people as Edward Carpenter, Karl Heinrich Ulrichs, John Addington Symonds, We'wha, BarCheeAmpe, Walt Whitman, Angelina Weld Grimke, Magnus Hirshfeld, Gertrude Stein, Alice B. Toklas, Oscar Wilde, Radclyffe Hall, Una Troubridge, Alice Dunbar-Nelson, Zora Neale Hurston, Langston Hughes, James Baldwin, and W. H. Auden.[9] Oftentimes we have to uncover lives that have been buried or gone unnoticed; and at other times we have to dig deeply into the lives of well-known people for details that have been hidden, forgotten, or neglected. Our tradition seems to be characterized more by "research into" than by "handing over." Gloria T. Hull's work, "'Under The Days': The Buried Life and Poetry of Angelina Weld Grimke," is an example of the effort and determination that are necessary if we are to build and recognize a tradition, if we are to remember, listen to, observe, and receive support from our people. Although many of these people were writers, my attention here is not focused so much on their writings or on literary criticism but on their lives. Letters, memoirs, biography, and autobiography are the sources of information that lend their lives to us.

Tradition is shaped by the process of their handing over and our receiving, by the interface of their and our different situations, by what we do and do not have in common with them. Sometimes I simply appreciate, take courage from, and observe how they lived; other times I see a model for what I want to do now. Mostly, though, I neither look for nor find inspiration and example; I simply find company, feel less alone and more a part of other people's lives.[10]

I do not take up and wear their lives as much as I find comfort, strength, and rest among them. I am as likely to marvel at their courage and progressive practices as I am to wish they had done more, been more open. I cannot help but bring my own agenda and bias to my observations of them. But I see the fault of such ahistorical visiting upon the past, and I am not preoccupied with making them fit my expectations or me fit theirs. Sometimes I find great sadness and tragedy in their lives and feel that instead of drawing support from them, I sit with them so that they are no longer alone, frightened, destroyed. I do not look for heroes, but simply find that household or neighborhood of ancestors with whom I laugh, scream, argue, cry, and feel at home, with those who dared to take themselves seriously enough to live against or in spite of social expectations. I fit into a past that continues through me into the present. I gain familiarity with those who cared for themselves in ways that give me, perhaps without their having intended to, some bearings, caring, and feeling of belonging.

EXPERIENCE

Just as I attempt to intensify the personal recognition and formation of Scripture and tradition, I am less inclined here to talk about the experiences of others and turn instead to explore my own experiences, especially those that are most private, hidden, deepest. The basis and source for knowing myself most intimately are the experiences and desires of my body, what Audre Lorde calls "the erotic—the sensual—those physical, emotional, and psychic expressions of what is deepest and strongest and richest within each of us."[11]

Christian theology typically separates body and mind, flesh and spirit, female and male, and privileges mind/spirit/male.[12] Christian ethicist Beverly Harrison observes that this "tendency of Christian theological tradition to neglect, ignore, or denigrate the body" sacralizes "mental activity or consciousness as 'higher' than the rest of physical existence":

> We are conditioned . . . to view the body and bodily needs as *"lower," "animal"* modalities of existence that have to be tamed or in some way overcome and transcended by a higher and loftier power that is *"really"* rational and spiritual. This assumption of a tension between what is most deeply *"spiritual"* and our physical embodiment and physical needs runs so deep in Christian culture that accepting the priority of mind over body, as if mind is not a function of body experienced in a certain way, or the *"transcendence"* of spirit over nature, is often held to be the essence of religious conviction. *"To believe"* comes to mean believing such nonsense. To be religious then involves living and acting as though a split between lower *"nature"* and consciousness were a part of fundamental reality.[13]

Lorde says, "We have been raised to fear the yes within ourselves, our deepest cravings," "to distrust that power which rises from our deepest and nonrational knowledge." We have been taught "to suspect this resource, vilified, abused, and devalued within western society."[14]

We have been "warned against it all our lives by the male world," because when we "recognize our deepest feelings," when we are "in touch with the power of the erotic within ourselves," we begin to give up suffering and self-negation, we "become less willing to accept powerlessness, or those other supplied states of being which are not native to [us], such as resignation, despair, self-effacement, depression, self-denial." When we understand and know our "capacity for joy," we come to expect and demand that same depth of satisfaction and joy throughout our daily life—in our jobs, in school, at home. When we allow the power of the erotic "projected from within us" to "inform and illuminate our actions upon the world around us," we will not "settle for the convenient, the shoddy, the conventionally expected, nor the merely safe." We may rebel, refuse, resist, assert, take, give. [15]

To be in touch with the erotic is neither solipsistic nor simply feeling good, for "in order to be utilized, our erotic feelings must be recognized [by others]. The need for sharing deep feeling is a human need." [16] The awkwardness of talking about my body and cravings, the fear of being considered self-centered and self-indulgent, and the anxiety about making myself too open and vulnerable signal to me the terrifying need to be explicit, to make the scary leap to reveal myself, to take seriously what I have so conveniently relegated to the realm of being less important than "normal" expressions of joy, love, relationship, fulfillment. How well I have acceded to the importance of weddings, anniversaries, biological family, and how willing I have been to remain silent about my own preferred ways of sharing my body, my feelings, my life! How difficult it is to remember that only in taking one's own life seriously can one be neighbor, lover, helper. As Dag Hammarskjold advises:

Hunger is my native place in the land of passions. . . .

And this hunger of mine can be satisfied for the simple reason that the nature of life is such that I can realize my individuality by becoming a bridge for others. . . .

Don't be afraid of yourself, live your individuality to the full—but for the good of others. Don't copy others in order to buy fellowship, or make convention your law instead of living the righteousness.

To become free and responsible. For this alone was [hu]man created, and he [or she] who fails to take the Way which could have been his [or hers] shall be lost eternally. [17]

Socially, I know the risk of revealing too much about ourselves. Discretion and caution are safer. Personally, I know that we must take that risk if we are really to know and care about each other. Candor and depth help us do that. As Lorde says, "If one Black woman I do not know gains hope and strength from my story, then it has been worth the difficulty of telling."[18]

My Deep and Nonrational Knowledge

When I was a child, categories of male and female, masculine and feminine, frightened me—most pointedly when Christine Jorgensen came to my small, New England resort town as a nightclub act, a singer. Made famous by her transsexual operation, Jorgensen was for the next two weeks the buzz of conversations that I overheard among my various adult relatives. And it terrified me; for the message, quite clearly, was that one was either a man or a woman, and if not, had to be made into one. I wanted to be neither. I simply wanted to live my life and do the things I wanted to do without their being appropriately male or female, the province of men or women. But of course I was learning that life—that is, life as ordered in my society—was not simple but unnaturally simplistic, not allowing for the complexity or disorder that I threatened to contribute and that I was afraid meant I must be crazy.

If you were to ask what precisely it was that I was feeling or doing at the time that told me I was beyond social expectations, I would find it hard to tell you. It had nothing to do with dressing in women's clothes, acting like a girl, or being effeminate. There were boys who were stigmatized for that; I was not one of them. Perhaps it would have been easier to understand myself if I had been. I was not asocial, socially unpleasant, or physically unattractive. I could and did play sports, I was accepted by my peers, and I fit in with the activities prescribed by the adults in my extended family. I could and did do it all, but it held little meaning for me. I did not feel involved. I cannot explain to you why I felt odd, deviant, or out of place, except to say that I knew my life was supposed to unfold and that I was supposed to act in a certain way that held no interest for me, that I was to become a man, a husband to a wife, and that together we would have children. Yet, violating that clear understanding of what my future was to be was my knowing that it was the last thing that I either wanted to do or was interested in doing. What would I have chosen to be? I have and had no idea. I only knew that what was expected was not what I would have chosen. I felt the urge to choose, select, pursue interests, but there was little or nothing available from which I could choose or with which I could identify that felt genuine.

I can remember only this hint of a model of what might have been. I hated Little League baseball, and after enduring two nervous seasons of trying to meet the expectations of a devoted baseball family, I did not bring home the registration forms when they were handed out at school the next year. I did not mention it at home, but of course my parents found out after a while. When they asked why, I told them I wanted to do something else. We went to visit an old farmer. He was an opinionated old Swamp Yankee who told the same stories again and again. Each time I listened attentively. I could not get enough of his ornery ways. He criticized wealthy, phony airs, and new-fangled ideas. I thought he was perfect; no one else shared my enthusiasm. He was considered a crotchety old man, and people avoided him and being detained by his rambling yarns. But my parents knew how important he was to me, and they made sure that our family schedule included regular and frequent time for me to go and work with him on his farm. I think I needed his oddness—to match my own, to spare me, relieve me from the overwhelming oddness I felt at home and school. None of this was explicit or intentional. I think I was simply finding a balance that allowed me to maintain, to survive, to get on without feeling abnormal.

If I seem to be struggling for a way to prove that I knew what I knew, or at least suspected it then, I am. There was no measure or sign that gave form or expression to what I felt. But I shall propose here a way to understand the predicament of gender that I experienced as a prepubescent youth, and to lend some substance to what may seem a vague and insubstantial memory of the past.

MY BODY OF EXPERIENCE, MY EXPERIENCE OF BODY

What I had suspected and predicted as a preteen was to become formalized in my experiences of reaching puberty. My childhood was by most standards an ideal one. My parents were the kind who took on themselves the responsibility of explaining the facts of life to their children. Sex, bodies, and physical love were accepted, enjoyed, and discussed openly by what were, I think, the most progressive standards. One Saturday, without embarrassment and with clear intention, my father made sure that I understood how human reproduction occurred. When he finished explaining how a wife and husband made love, I remember blurting out, "Do they have to?" and was assured that they indeed want to. I was not convinced but thought something was going to happen to me that would change all that. Soon after, just before leaving for college, my older brother—at the request of my parents, I am sure—had a discussion with me about masturbation. He said that when I was fourteen I would start to masturbate, that it was a fine thing to do, our parents would not mind; and he explained how it was done. He said that while I was doing it I would be thinking about girls. I thought, "Great, this is the big change I've been waiting for." So, on the night of my fourteenth birthday I masturbated, trying to think about girls, but I was really more occupied with the mechanics of the process. Subsequently, as I continued to masturbate, without making any clear decision to do so, I found myself thinking less about girls and more about boys—indeed, the most satisfying times involved fantasies about boys and men—and masturbation became for me exclusively and satisfactorily homoerotic.

I did not know anything about fellatio or anal sex, the so-called practices of homosexuality. Masturbating had nothing to do with being a female or a male, of being feminine or masculine. I did not even know the word "homosexuality." I had nothing to copy or imitate. I was charting my private journey without a map. And my guide was quite simply a yearning for the touch, feel, and excitement of male skin, of a male body, against my own. It did not even have much to do with genitals; it had to do with holding, caressing, embracing, feeling a whole body against mine. And the imagined scenarios were laden with a sense of comfort, protection, and gentleness. That is what I yearned for and created in my fantasies. My only resource for creating it, my only resource for knowing that it could exist, was an ache for shared pleasure, my body and my feelings, what they demanded, what they knew. My body was letting me know, confirming, that there had been something to the unsettled and suspicious feelings of my preteen years. My body gave evidence, substantiated, formalized, gave expression to that earlier uncertainty—that I wanted/needed to do something that was unexpected and not taught. In spite of social expectations, gender-role socialization, and sex education, my body was determined to have its way; and my decision was, in my fantasies at least, to go with it, to imagine what was not permitted or even available as a model, while living out my daily life as a normal, happy heterosexual adolescent.

I have since found out in conversations with others that I was not the only one. I turn to Scripture, specifically to E. M. Forster's novel *Maurice*, for a scene that replicates my own and captures a situation, experience, or set of feelings that other gay men hold in common.

Finding Acceptance, Finding Scripture

Forster's clearly stated intention was to write/create/present that which was not thought possible or right. Writing in 1960 about the novel, which had been written in 1913 and 1914, he said: "A happy ending was imperative. I shouldn't have bothered to write otherwise. I was determined that in fiction anyway two men should fall in love and remain in it for the ever and ever that fiction allows, and in this sense Maurice and Alec still roam the greenwood. I dedicated it 'To a Happier Year' and not altogether vainly. Happiness is its keynote."[19]

If you have read *Maurice*, or seen the movie,[20] you may remember the scene in which the well-intentioned schoolmaster takes aside the young fatherless Maurice to tell him about sex, love, and life. Walking with Maurice on the beach, the teacher explains "scientifically and sympathetically." He draws diagrams in the sand, and the novel reads that Maurice

> *watched dully: it bore no relation to his experiences. . . . He knew that the subject was serious and related to his own body. But he could not himself relate it; it fell to pieces as soon as [the teacher] put it together, like an impossible sum. In vain he tried. His torpid brain would not awake.*

And rather than entertain the possibility that it might be beyond the concern, interest, or comprehension of Maurice, the teacher rationalizes Maurice's nonresponse as the reserve and "cultivated feelings" of a young man raised to be a gentleman; he does "not realize that [Maurice] must either understand nothing or be overwhelmed." The clues are there, but the teacher won't or cannot see them. Maurice does not ask the "kind of question" that boys had asked him in the past; he merely says, "I see, I see, I see." So the teacher quizzes him, and Maurice's "replies were satisfactory." He even knows enough to demonstrate "a spurious intelligence, a surface flicker to respond to the beaconing glow of the [teacher's]." With relief, the teacher could then say, "'That's right. . . . You need never be puzzled or bothered now." He then could move on to discuss love and life:

> *To love a noble woman, to protect and serve her—this, he told the little boy, was the crown of life. . . . "It all hangs together—all— and God's in his heaven, All's right with the world. Male and female! Ah wonderful!"*

And like my response to my father's scientific, sympathetic, well-intended explanation, Maurice says, "I think I shall not marry." And then comes the trump card, the final persuasion, the not-so-subtle coercion—the teacher says:

> *"This day ten years hence—I invite you and your wife to dinner with my wife and me. Will you accept?"*
> *"Oh sir!" [Maurice] smiled with pleasure.*

*"It's a bargain, then!" [says the teacher]. . . . Maurice was flat-
tered and began to contemplate the marriage.*

But the feeling holds only until the teacher looks back and sees some
people, including "a lady," approach the place where he had made
the drawings in the sand and remembers with panic, "I never
scratched out those infernal diagrams." And the episode closes with:
*And suddenly for an instant of time, the boy despised [the teacher].
"Liar," he thought. "Liar, coward, he's told me nothing." . . .
Then darkness rolled up again, the darkness that is primeval but not
eternal, and yields to its own painful dawn.*

There is within this scenario a mixture of what I had experienced:
The clear message of what I was supposed to do, the lack of understanding of its application to me—and the gap, the glimpse, the
crack through which some element of rescue could bring me to my
senses, to an awareness of my body and its feelings. Like Maurice's,
my body was living in a secret night, but one that yielded to a dawn,
albeit a temporary, fleeting, and painful one.[21]

Maurice's story then unfolds with the familiar net of strategies
of camouflage, deception, and discretion known to most gay men.
And the history of the novel's publication itself is not exempt from
those same concerns. Forster wrote in 1960 that the keynote of
happiness in *Maurice*

*had an unexpected result: it . . . made the book more difficult to
publish. Unless the Wolfenden Report [in Britain] becomes law, it
will probably have to remain in manuscript. If it had ended unhap-
pily, with a lad dangling from a noose or with a suicide pact, all
would be well. . . . But the lovers get away unpunished and conse-
quently recommend crime.[22]*

But contrary to those social conditions and personal strategies, the
character of Maurice created by Forster is about change, transformation, salvation. Into the "handsome, healthy, bodily attractive,
mentally torpid, not a bad business man and rather a snob," Forster
says he "dropped an ingredient that puzzles him, wakes him up,

torments him and finally saves him. His surroundings exasperate him by their very normality: mother, two sisters, a comfortable home, a respectable job gradually turn out to be Hell; he must either smash them or be smashed, there is no third course." And for Forster "the working out of such a character, the setting of traps for him which he sometimes eluded, sometimes fell into, and finally did smash, proved a welcome task."[23]

I find myself and am accepted in this story; it is as much about me as about Maurice. But *Maurice* puts me in touch, also, with the third resource for theological reflection—tradition.

FINDING COMPANY IN TRADITION

Edward Carpenter (1844-1929) was a poet, social reformer, and critic who wrote about a wide range of social issues. He left an upper-middle-class, Cambridge-educated background to live among the working class in northern England, and he played a major role in the socialist revival of the 1880s and in the national drive to establish a party of Labour. His book *Towards Democracy* was a "kind of bible" for these movements, as well as a poetic celebration of the love of men for men, women for women, and of men for women and women for men "on a newer greater scale than it had hitherto been conceived." On his cooperative farm at Milthorpe, he met and set up a home with his lover, George Merrill, a working-class man from Sheffield. In the words of later-day biographer Noel Greig, he "was to establish, in a practical sort of way, the comrade-love of which he had sung in his poems, had yearned for all his life." He continued to go out to lecture and to support certain causes, but his developing personal life with Merrill became the focus of his work from then on. Within the context of their relationship and work together on the farm, "his writings [began] to reflect his meditations on the nature of personal relations and sexuality—and a great deal of trouble they caused him, too."[24]

After the arrest of Oscar Wilde in 1895, Carpenter's publisher reneged on a contract to issue his new work, *Love's Coming of Age*, even though it was not about homosexuality. According to Carpenter, "a sheer panic prevailed over *all* questions of sex." The publisher was also afraid of associations that would be made with a pamphlet titled *Homogenic Love*, which Carpenter had printed and circulated privately—"Even in this quiet way the pamphlet created some alarm—and . . . caused no little fluttering and agitation." His publisher also refused to continue selling *Towards Democracy*. Carpenter later recalled:

> In '96 no "*respectable*" *publisher would touch [*Love's Coming of Age]. . . . The severe resistance and rigidity of public opinion at the time made the volume very difficult to write. . . . Nearly every chapter in the book was written four or five times over before I was satisfied with it.*

But Carpenter, bolstered by the aesthetic movement that had formed around Wilde, and by the contemporary work of John Addington Symonds, Havelock Ellis, K. H. Ulrichs, and Magnus Hirschfeld, did continue to write essays about homosexuality. These were eventually published as *The Intermediate Sex* in 1908. His language and approach remained tentative and cautious; and he did not come out openly as homosexual in his writing until *My Days and Dreams*, published in 1916. By this time, some suggest, he was protected from scandal and criticism by old age. But his work was received and reviewed with much appreciation by lesbians and gay men in America and Europe. *The Intermediate Sex* was reprinted regularly and, according to Greig, "remained for several decades the most positive text available in English from which gay people could draw support and hope."[25]

And for thirty years—from 1898 until Merrill's death—Carpenter did live openly with his lover at Milthorpe, an influential and supportive gathering spot for many visitors and friends. Their union was not without risk in a social climate of enforced heterosexual conformity and proved a source of both difficulty and support for those around them. In their pursuit of respectability and mainstream politics, some colleagues in the Labour movement rejected

Carpenter. "If the Fates pointed favourably I need hardly say that my friends (with a few exceptions) pointed the other way!" Forster was one of those exceptions.[26]

He tells us that *Maurice* was "the direct result of a visit to the seventy-year-old Carpenter" in 1914. After describing Carpenter's political and social activities, Forster says Carpenter "was a believer in the Love of Comrades. . . . It was this last aspect that attracted me in my loneliness. For a short time he seemed to hold the key to every trouble. I approached him . . . as one approaches a saviour."[27]

Forster recalls that on one of his visits Merrill "touched my backside—gently and just above the buttocks. . . . The sensation was unusual and I still remember it. . . . It was as much psychological as physical. It seemed to go straight through the small of my back into my ideas, without involving my thoughts. . . . I then returned to Harrogate . . . and immediately began to write *Maurice*. No other of my books has started off this way. The general plan, the three characters, the happy ending for two of them, all rushed into my pen. And the whole thing went through without a hitch." Alec, the working-class character who saves Maurice, "starts as an emanation from Milthorpe, he is the touch on the backside."[28]

SAVED BY A RIOT OF BUTCH DYKES AND RAGING QUEENS

There is within each of the resources for theological reflection and formation that I have discussed an awareness, recognition, and even practice of a knowledge that comes from within—from the body, its touch, feelings, and need for relationship—and that survives and is expressed via some protective or camouflaging strategy, in spite of social disapproval and restrictions. I did, for example, find an affectional relationship with my Yankee farmer that offset the oddness I felt as a child, and my desire for the touch of men took form and was expressed through my imagination and masturbation as an adolescent. Forster's desire for a happy ending took form and found expression in the company of "comrades" and through the touch by one of them, which was preserved in fiction but not published in his lifetime. And Carpenter's ideas and research on homosexuality found their most explicit expression and development in the context of his relationship and home with Merrill—not without caution, struggle, and opposition for a time, but more freely in old age and rural isolation.

If each of my resources helps me to recognize, describe, and explain what is most important to me, each also fails to explain why I am able to work and write today as an openly gay theologian, to interact with students as an openly gay professor, and to live openly with a man in a primary affectional/sexual relationship. Nor have I explained my access to Forster's *Maurice* and Carpenter's life and work; for neither was among the literature, history, and tradition available or included in my formal education and upbringing. *Maurice* was not published until after Forster's death in 1970; and Carpenter, by Forster's own admission on a BBC radio show in 1944, had been mostly forgotten.[29] Each resource recognizes the existence and restricted exercise of knowledge, but none embodies it, gives it concrete form, endures. Each resource lacks its own ability to sustain itself. Each, as discussed, works or needs to hide, protect, or cover that knowledge. A single historical event, what I designate as a salvific event, was to alter their social invisibility.

A routine police raid on a gay/lesbian bar occurred on June 27, 1969, in Greenwich Village in New York City. But as patrons were ejected from the Stonewall Inn and directed toward paddy wagons by the local police, "they erupted with unexpected outrage and rioted for at least four nights." The rioters used "hit-and-run tactics reminiscent of guerilla warfare; the police responded with its special riot unit."[30] At Stonewall an assortment of butch lesbians, Puerto Rican drag queens, and effeminate gay men—marginal people even within their own marginalized population—led charges against rows of uniformed police officers. Their courage proved infectious. By June of the following year, ten thousand marched to celebrate the first anniversary of that rebellion; by 1975 anniversary events were occurring in dozens of cities; within four years the number of organizations for lesbians and gay men nationally had grown from fifty to more than eight hundred; by the end of the 1970s the number of organizations was in the thousands.[31]

Whether we wanted it to or not, this event changed the lives of lesbian/gay/bisexual people. Stonewall was the irreversible deliverance from accepting silence, invisibility, and victimhood. It so accurately addressed our needs that we could not avoid it; it thrilled and shocked us, relieved and frightened us. It was the act of resistance, anger, and violence that so many had wanted to express but never thought possible. It became the possible "No" that would be rehearsed and repeated by lesbians and gay men as they began to deal with friends, parents, jobs, church, and government in new ways. But it also pushed us, forced us into the new possibility, let us know that there were no excuses. Freedom was not handed to us; the possibility of it was. Each of us had to take on a bit of the terror that comes when charging against the rows of authority; we had to experience the fear of risking security and embracing unfamiliar and uncertain freedom.

> *The whole congregation of the people of Israel murmured against Moses and Aaron in the wilderness, and said to them, "Would that we had died by the hand of the Lord in the land of Egypt, when we sat by the fleshpots and ate bread to the full; for you have brought us out into this wilderness to kill this whole assembly with hunger."* (Exod. 16:2-3)[32]

But because in a very ordinary situation a few very unlikely leaders had done the very unexpected, we would never be in Egypt again and could not return there. The doors of our closeted lives had been blown off, and since that time it has been the responsibility of each of us to take advantage of the possibility of finding our way out of those closets. Stonewall was not a once-and-for-all event but one that is relived daily. As Eve Kosofsky Sedgwick observes in *Epistemology of the Closet*:

> *Even at the individual level, there are remarkably few of even the most openly gay people who are not deliberately in the closet with someone personally or economically or institutionally important to*

them. Furthermore, the deadly elasticity of heterosexist presumption means that, like Wendy in Peter Pan, people find new walls springing up around them even as they drowse: every encounter with a new classful of students, to say nothing of a new boss, social worker, loan officer, landlord, doctor, erects new closets whose fraught and characteristic laws of optics and physics exact from at least gay people new surveys, new calculations, new draughts and requisitions of secrecy or disclosure. Even an out gay person deals daily with interlocutors about whom she doesn't know whether they know or not; it is equally difficult to guess for any given interlocutor whether, if they did know, the knowledge would seem very important. Nor—at the most basic level—is it unaccountable that someone who wanted a job, custody or visiting rights, insurance, protection from violence, from "therapy," from distorting stereotype, from insulting scrutiny, from simple insult, from forcible interpretation of their bodily product, could deliberately choose to remain in or to reenter the closet in some or all segments of their life. The gay closet is not a feature only of the lives of gay people. But for many gay people it is still the fundamental feature of social life; and there can be few gay people, however courageous and forthright by habit, however fortunate in the support of their immediate communities, in whose lives the closet is not still a shaping presence. [33]

We struggle still in the wilderness, but with the confidence that we are not alone. Stonewall is our source of encouragement and possibility; and Stonewall is repeated as we continue to face down threats, solve problems, and move beyond barriers.

In 1971, two years after Stonewall, at the age of twenty-six, I came out as a gay man and began the process of living openly in the various areas of my life—with friends and lovers, at work, with my biological family, and in the church. Forster's *Maurice* was first published in 1971, issued as a paperback in 1981, and made into a movie in 1987. [34] The post-Stonewall decades have also been a time in which lesbian and gay scholars have begun to research and claim a past that we did not know existed. Greig says that he "first stumbled upon Edward Carpenter in 1977—as a footnote [—while] researching a play which dealt, in part, with Victorian attitudes towards homosexuality."[35] That gay men and lesbians have stood, acted, and written noticeably in the past no doubt sustains, relieves, encourages, and inspires me and others; but that past was not handed to or passed on to us. We have had to go looking for it, resurrect it, and pass it on. The project of reclaiming our ancestors would not have happened without the courage and confidence born in the post-Stonewall liberation movement.

Martin Luther King, Jr., said that "it is an axiom of social change that no revolution can take place without a methodology suited to the circumstances of that period."[36] For us that method was physical violence by those most willing to violate standards of gender. I write, work, study, live, and love as a gay man today because in 1969 raging dykes and queens used their bodies to resist, oppose, and break the hold of the forces that had kept my body and my knowledge of it silent.

8
Credo:
The Creative and Saving
Spirit of Community

FAMILIAR TERMS WITH NEW MEANINGS

I CLOSE WITH A STATEMENT of belief and understanding that relies on and interprets familiar Trinitarian terms—God the Creator, Jesus the Savior, and the Spirit of Community. I also use the categories of sin, salvation, and grace; crucifixion and resurrection; and the sacraments of baptism and the meal to organize and articulate my beliefs.

GOD THE CREATOR

I believe that we are created and destroyed in our relationships. God is the mutuality and reciprocity in our relationships, the compelling and transforming power that brings together, reconciles, and creates us. The creative power of mutuality and the destruction wrought by its absence are perhaps most readily and urgently represented by the "non-negotiable demands" that we humans are getting "right now from the air, the water, the soil." As poet Gary Snyder warns:

*A culture that alienates itself from the very ground of its own
being—from the wilderness outside and from that other wilderness,
the wilderness within—is doomed to a very destructive behavior, ultimately perhaps self-destructive behavior.*

Within a "realm of life" that includes "animals, humans, and a
variety of wild life," we are created and sustained by "the interaction
of water, air, and soil" as well as by what humans do to and for others.[1]

However, I have come to know, believe in, and understand
God as mutuality-in-relationship mostly because of my interpersonal
experiences, whether in the physical intimacy and exchanges of yes
and no with my lover or in my job, where my gifts are received and
considered important as much as I receive and value the gifts of
others. I have become and am becoming fully human because of
those relationships—social, sexual, political, economic—in which
I both take seriously and am taken seriously by others, in which we
need and depend on one another, in which we initiate and follow,
welcome and are welcomed, challenge and are challenged, encourage and are encouraged, take risks and find rest. My understanding
of God as mutuality-in-relationship has a basis also in Hebrew and
Christian Scripture.

Yahweh is often portrayed as covenant maker, as one who
makes or renews an agreement with his troubled children. Yahweh
also sometimes arranges and coordinates agreements between people. God initiates, establishes, and directs relationships with and
among us.[2]

In the books of 1 and 2 Samuel, however, Jonathan and David
first make their covenant without any direct reference to Yahweh,
and later they renew it before Yahweh. In this case God is neither
a party to the covenant nor a facilitator of it; instead, God is the
love and comfort that Jonathan and David exchange and depend on.
Jonathan's love for David is Yahweh's action, not the result of
Yahweh's directions. This love is not initiated, made, or directed by
Yahweh; the love as it is shared and needed by David and Jonathan
and as it changes and creates them in their relationship is Yahweh.

God is not the facilitator of mutuality but is the mutuality itself: "Yahweh shall be between me and you for ever."[3]

My equating of God with mutuality and reciprocity is sustained also by the Song of Songs and by what Jesus called the greatest commandment.

In the Book of Genesis, Yawheh creates biological woman and man in Eden, withdraws to let them enjoy their relationship, and intervenes only to punish them when they violate mutuality (woman for being too assertive or dominant, man for being too passive or submissive). So, also, Yahweh as administrator remains absent when lovers discover themselves in intimacy and recover mutuality in the garden of eroticism in the Song of Songs—"My lover is mine, and I am his."[4] God is present and creative as mutuality in the relationship, not as an outside party who directs and manages it. In relationship, mutuality creates the lovers as equal, free of stereotypes and gender roles in lovemaking or work, bold and open in expressing desire, and as likely to approach as be approached by the other.[5]

When asked what is "the great" or "the first" commandment, Jesus says it is to love God totally and to love your neighbor as yourself: "One is the great and first commandment, and the second is like it."[6] The simultaneity, equality, and unity of these two commandments lead me to understand God as "within our midst," as the accepting, the interacting, and the loving that go on in the neighborhood and make it an open, diverse, inclusive, productive community. God is the-loving-of-the-other-as-you-want-to-be-loved that creates a community in which the gifts and talents of all are welcome, developed, considered special.

I understand God not as above, other, or outside but as among, between, and part of us. To describe my God is to describe what happens between us that makes us good, makes us more fully human, makes our lives ultimately meaningful. Lesbian-feminist theologian Carter Heyward, who has done the pioneering and most extensive work on mutual relation, advises: "Don't be duped by folks who talk about 'God' all the time. It's more critical to make the connections among ourselves. And a hell of a lot more honest."[7] The connections among ourselves—the often awkward, difficult, challenging, satisfying, comforting, nurturing, thrilling demands that we put on and experience with each other—are God making us, creating us as fully human.

SIN

Sin is the violation of mutuality and reciprocity, typically in the form of dominance and submission. Sin is the exercise of power over others that compromises their living fully. We recognize sin as the institutionalized denial of equal opportunity, participation, and representation in the social order. Examples are the lack of affordable housing and widespread homelessness, the failure to pass equal rights legislation for women, economic privileges for the wealthy and lower standards of living for some people, and unilateral decision making by powerful nations and their intervention in the affairs of small ones. Sin is also interpersonal violation, such as the neglect of children, domestic violence, rape, and bias-related violence.

In the Bible, Yahweh responds to the sin of slavery in Egypt, the prophets Amos and Micah denounce material excess at the expense of the poor, and Jesus counters the prevailing exclusion and silencing of people;[8] but elsewhere sexual violence against women is treated benignly, and in some of his letters Paul accommodates slavery and encourages women's submission to men.[9] The Bible is not a coherent rule book with a consistent, reliable, and currently applicable list of sins, but it does provide some guidelines for naming and changing what is wrong. The Exodus reminds us that pain and suffering inflicted upon one person or a people by another is unacceptable and should be changed. The prophets call on us to "let justice roll down like waters," "to do justice, to love kindness." Jesus reminds us to welcome the outcast, to love our neighbor as ourself, to listen to those we are least likely to take seriously.[10]

We may need these reminders, because blaming the victim, not listening to stories of pain and suffering, and seeing only from our own viewpoint may let us avoid discovering our own complicity, feeling our own responsibility, and realizing our ability to respond to and solve problems. We may also need to be reminded and encouraged to speak of our own pain, to insist that our own needs be met, to ask for and insist on being helped.

Churches and denominations need to be reminded that when they ask lesbians/bisexual/gay clergy to be celibate, to refrain from practicing or expressing their sexual preference/orientation, they are telling people what they want them to do and are not listening to what people need to do. The oft-repeated cop-out to "hate the sin, not the sinner," to hate homosexuality not homosexuals, conveniently avoids the real sin, which is preventing people from becoming fully human, from living as fully sexual, affectional, active humans.

And lesbians and gay men need to be reminded that to submit, to do as we are told, not to speak out, not to act up, not to live openly, not to become fully human is sinful, also. As Audre Lorde says:

> *For me, living fully means living with maximum access to my experience and power, loving, and doing work in which I believe. It means writing my poems, telling my stories, and speaking out of my most urgent concerns and against the many forms of anti-life surrounding us.* [11]

Although I am inclined to consider acts of silencing, abusing, and neglecting others as more blameworthy than remaining silent or accepting abuse or neglect, the latter are as sinful and as in need of change. To submit is as sinful as to dominate.

SALVATION AND GRACE

Salvation is to protest and resist the exercise of nonmutual, nonreciprocal power; to replace unjust relationship with partnership, cooperation, sharing, and exchange; to include people and to recognize differences as a resource for building meaningful relationships rather than as the basis for the unequal distribution of power.

Salvation is "to choose *your* self," not to "be afraid of yourself," to "live your individuality to the full—but for the good of others." Dag Hammarskjold says:

> *Body and soul contain a thousand possibilities out of which you can build many I's. But in only one of them is there a congruence of the elector and the elected. Only one—which you will never find until*

you have excluded all those superficial and fleeting possibilities of being and doing with which you toy, out of curiosity or wonder or greed, and which hinder you from casting anchor in the experience of the mystery of life, and the consciousness of the talent entrusted to you which is your I.[12]

Each of us is favored or graced with talents or gifts. As Paul writes in his Letter to the Romans, "Having gifts that differ according to the grace given to us, let us use them."[13] In recognizing, developing, and exercising our talents—in giving our gifts—we save ourselves and others from indifference, apathy, and death. We give and receive life. We embrace, allow, foster our creation as fully human.

Audre Lorde speaks of talent, favor, or grace as privilege, and she recognizes also that our talents do not have to be used to separate or order some of us as better than others but are the resource for connecting us with each other.

To acknowledge privilege is the first step in making it available for wider use. Each of us is blessed in some particular way, whether we recognize our blessings or not. And each of us, somewhere in our lives, must clear a space within that blessing where she can call upon whatever resources are available to her in the name of something that must be done.[14]

Salvation is to stake one's life on our ability and need to give to and receive from others. It is to be included, recognized, and valued, to overcome being either dominant or submissive, to share power with others.

But one cannot set out to save or be saved by others. Salvation is not a program and cannot be strategized. It cannot be designed, planned, or shaped by purpose or intent. We cannot make others receive our gifts, nor can we make them give us theirs. To save others is not to instruct them, but to listen to them or help them hear you. We cannot know and decide to do what is best for others as much as we can be available by being who we are and letting others be who they are. The rebels of Stonewall did not show or tell us how to act; instead, in acting as they needed to act they gave us the permission and encouragement to act as we need to act, each of us in our own situation, in our own closet, in our time, at our own pace. We cannot model or show others what they should do as much as we can encourage others to be themselves by being ourselves, by doing what we need to do without apology or excuse.

The power of salvation, what Hammarskjold refers to as "the mystery of life," is that we cannot predict when or know how our lives lived openly may affect or save others. Salvific moments are unexpected, come unannounced, and occur in ordinary circumstances. That Rosa Parks, an ordinary, tired, workingwoman, would change the world by sitting down in the "wrong" part of a bus was neither planned, predicted, nor expected. We cannot explain why this person, at this time, doing this act had the power to affect the lives of so many. We only know that these moments happen, that we save one another when we live among each other doing what we need to do and saying what we need to say.

The lack of control that we have over the outcome and impact of living fully and openly among others is readily understood by lesbians and gay men through the process of coming out. Most of us have struggled with the difficulties of asserting ourselves, becoming more visible, and contributing our point of view and talents to the society at large. We know that coming out is both scary and rewarding, that we are both supported and rebuked, and that the process is never over. We know that we confide in people who listen to us and hear us into our coming out. And we know also that our seeing and hearing about other people's coming out helps us to make our own moves. We often see and hear them from our own safe distance; and they save us, give us strength, provide an example and encouragement without knowing they do so. Coming out is intensely individual, explicitly personal, but it has social implications and affects others in ways that one cannot foresee or know for sure.

Those who may respond to us most demonstrably or vociferously are probably not the ones whom we save. The outspoken parent, teacher, or boss who disowns or welcomes, attacks or defends, discredits or praises is not the one we save. It is more likely the quiet nephew, neighbor, and coworker, watching and listening in the background or even hearing secondhand, who take the news and store it up for their own salvation, their own coming out.

We know that our coming out affects other people, but we cannot control who will be affected or how they will be affected. Certain ways or actions do not guarantee certain effects. We cannot plan or shape our coming out to maximize its effect on others. We can only come out with regard for the talents, gifts, favor, grace that have been entrusted to us. Only by living our individuality to the full, by anchoring ourselves in our own humanity, do we live for the good of others, become a bridge to others. And we do not always get to choose who those others may be or what form the goodness or bridge may take. We save and are saved by others when we insist on taking ourselves and others seriously. But we take ourselves and one another seriously without the purpose, expectation, or guarantee of saving others; we do this simply for the love of ourselves and the satisfaction of living fully among others. The moments of salvation come when most needed—not decided, planned, or arranged by us, but surprising, stretching, helping, changing, saving us.

JESUS THE SAVIOR: CRUCIFIXION AND RESURRECTION

To the poor, outcast, despised, neglected, and needy Jesus gave healing, affirmation, and voice. But those whom Jesus befriended do not make up a neatly defined social category. He also sat with, responded to, helped, and enjoyed the company of tax collectors, rulers, officials, and military commanders.[15] His life directs us to take seriously the gifts of all people.

But his message is not simply one-dimensional advice to be kind to and considerate of others. In his ministry, Jesus too was affirmed and given voice by those in whose midst he lived. Jesus found meaning in giving to and receiving from others. It was a nameless woman, scolded by some for wasting money by anointing him with costly oil, whom Jesus defended, saying: "Let her alone. Why do you trouble her? She has done a beautiful thing to me. . . . Truly, I say to you, wherever the gospel is preached in the whole world, what she has done will be told in memory of her."[16] Jesus, too, needed to have beautiful things done to him.

Although we are directed to the marginalized and encouraged to include others not like ourselves, we are also encouraged to insist on our own inclusion and recognition by others, to express ourselves, to count ourselves as one of those who needs to be heard and received by others. To borrow the words of lesbian/Chicana poet and essayist, Cherrie Moraga:[17]

> I am a welder.
> Not an alchemist.
> I am interested in the blend
> of common elements to make
> a common thing.
>
> No magic here.
> Only the heat of my desire to fuse
> what I already know
> exists. Is possible.

As Jesus was both received and given to and because the range of those whom he befriended was extensive and not narrow, we are invited not only to be the one who can do for others, but also the one who needs to be cared for. Our own pain and needs must be taken as seriously as we take those around us.

> For too long a time
> the heat of my heavy hands
> has been smoldering
> in the pockets of other
> people's business—
> they need oxygen to make fire.
>
> I am now
> coming up for air.
> Yes, I am
> picking up the torch.[18]

And just as Jesus was special not because he was set apart, but because he set himself among others, so we "save" and "are saved

by" others when we live in the midst of those who take us seriously
and are taken seriously by us:

> It is the intimacy of steel melting
> into steel, the fire of our individual
> passion to take hold of ourselves
> that makes sculpture of our lives,
> builds buildings.

> And I am not talking about skyscrapers,
> merely structures that can support us
> without fear
> of trembling.[19]

Our being saved is neither in acting like Jesus nor in adoring and
accepting him; it is in accepting and living with each other as if our
very lives depended on it.

The story of the crucifixion reminds us that including others
and insisting on being included is not a simple, easy task:

> We plead to each other
> we all come from the same rock
> we all come from the same rock
> ignoring the fact that we bend
> at different temperatures
> that each of us is malleable
> up to a point.

> Yes, fusion is possible
> but only if things get hot enough—
> all else is temporary adhesion,
> patching up.[20]

Cruel and great is the opposition to our efforts to break down
barriers, build bridges, overcome separation, and refuse to be submissive. We remember in the Book of Esther the price paid by Vashti
when she chose to remain with her women friends and refused to
come before the drunken king at his command. And we recognize
such vehement opposition in the common occurrence of antigay/

lesbian violence, the reaffirmation of exclusivity by most religious denominations, and the U.S. Supreme Court's approval of criminalizing same-sex relations.

The resurrection stories, however, remind us that even the most severe opposition does not have the power to prevent the impact of our efforts on others. Opposition cannot destroy the world-changing and meaningful effect of our efforts to reach out and be reached: Jonathan's love for David endured Saul's objections; Rosa Parks's disobedience inspired a surge in the movement for civil rights; raging queens and dykes at Stonewall dismantled a tradition of silence and fear; some denominations, municipalities, and courts have moved officially to recognize, welcome, and accept us as full members and citizens; and the U.S. Congress did pass legislation requiring that the federal government collect statistics on crimes motivated by sexual-orientation, race, ethnic, or religious bias. Opposition often causes us to define our love more clearly and stand by it more steadfastly:

> *I am the welder.*
> *I understand the capacity of heat*
> *to change the shape of things.*
> *I am suited to work*
> *within the realm of sparks*
> *out of control.*
>
> *I am the welder.*
> *I am taking the power*
> *into my own hands.*[21]

The building of bridges and inclusive, diverse communities is not easily achieved and does not happen simply because of our wish for harmony and unity.

Often we are stretched beyond our own expectations when we learn that the particular needs of others require adjusting our own outlook, behavior, and plans. Often, with the best of intentions, we listen selectively and do not hear the pain. Sometimes confrontation, conflict, anger, and shouting are the means by which we are challenged by or challenge others to see beyond "what is" to what needs to be done. Well-intending white people may have to squirm a bit when faced with their own racism. We all may have to face the closets we still inhabit. Our flattening of others and our inattention to their needs may have to be brought out and settled in a process of sparks flying, of argument and debate.[22]

When Jesus says that he has "not come to bring peace to the world" but "a sword" and "division," where foes will be of our own households, where a house will be divided and family members set against one another,[23] he sketches a scenario familiar to many lesbians and gay men who have come out in our denominations, workplaces, and families of origin. The eventual acceptance of us often occurs only after a long period of anxiety, hostility, shunning, silence, and denunciation. If we expected, counted on, and waited for a time when there would be a peaceful or tame resolution with our churches or families, we would probably never come out. We raise up ourselves with the kind of trembling, astonishment, and fear with which the women left the empty tomb on Easter morning.[24] And we sometimes have to be willing to be pushy, angry, and hotheaded, to fight and insist, to refuse and assert, if we are to be taken seriously and included.

THE SPIRIT OF COMMUNITY: BAPTISM AND THE MEAL

If God is understood as the mutuality and reciprocity in our relationships and Jesus is our saving one another from loneliness, despair, abuse, and neglect, the Holy Spirit is the community that includes and encourages each person to share her or his gifts. The "holy" or "whole" spirit—the creative and saving power of God set among us—is inclusive community. As Paul told the congregation at Corinth:

> Now there are varieties of gifts, but the same Spirit. . . . To each is given the manifestation of the Spirit for the common good. . . . All these [gifts] are inspired by one and the same Spirit. . . .
>
> For just as the body is one and has many members, and all the members of the body, though many, are one, so it is with Christ [or

community]. For by one Spirit we were all baptized into one body—
Jews or Greeks, slaves or free—and all were made to drink of one
Spirit.
  For the body does not consist of one member but of many. . . . If
all were a single organ, where would the body be? As it is, there are
many parts, yet one body. The eye cannot say to the hand, "I have
no need of you," nor again the head to the feet, "I have no need of
you." . . . If one member suffers, all suffer together; if one member
is honored, all rejoice together. (1 Cor. 12:4, 7, 11, 12-14, 19-21,
26)[25]

Such community does not expect to make all alike, to flatten
difference. It promises to be shaped by the particular needs and
differences of its members, not to shape and reduce them to sim-
ilarity. Such community promises welcome and nourishment for all
who want and need to share their lives.

In the church this unconditional welcome and nourishment are
formalized and passed along as the sacraments of baptism and the
meal. To be sure, these practices have been so particularized along
denominational lines as to be exclusive; but their original and
potential power and purpose to welcome, share, and nourish one
another deserve to be reclaimed if we are to build inclusive communities in which people lead meaningful lives. To inherit these
sacraments and to pass them on is to live forever. For to be welcomed
and to be nourished is to be sustained by those who come before us;
and to welcome and to nourish is to sustain those who will come after
us. To keep these sacraments alive so that others will continue to
be welcomed and nourished is to feel the spirit moving us toward
others and others toward us. Not to feel the spirit—not to be in and
building community—is to exclude and be excluded, to separate and
be separated, to deny others their humanity and to be denied one's
own, to kill others and be dead. To live forever is to nurture the
impulse of community to be ever expanding and inclusive.

Gary Snyder enlarges our understanding of body/church/ community by speaking of "the land—a country—[as] a region within
which the interactions of water, air, and soil and the underlying

geology and the overlying wind conditions all go to create both the microclimates and the large climatic patterns that make a whole sphere or realm of life possible." He challenges our inclusivity by identifying "the people" within this realm as "animals, humans, and a variety of wild life." And he advises us to find ways to "incorporate the other people—what the Sioux Indians called the creeping people, and the standing people, and the flying people, and the swimming people—into the councils of government." A conversation with John Lame Deer would suggest that to incorporate these other people may mean learning to listen and talk to owls and butterflies, or "to discover—a herb, a sprig, a flower—a very small flower, maybe, and you can spend a long time in its contemplation." Snyder suggests that "the possibilities of incorporating spokesmanship for the rest of life in our democratic society" lie in such intimate attempts to contemplate and communicate, to "become seized . . . by the spirit of the deer," to "impersonate the squash blossom," so that we are "no longer speaking *for* humanity," but "taking it on [our]selves to interpret, *through* [our] humanity, what these other life-forms [are]" (emphasis mine).[26] We need to recognize our new neighbors, to enlarge the dimensions of our neighborhood and love our new neighbors as we would love ourselves.

Notes

INTRODUCTION

1. Paul Tillich, *Dynamics of Faith* (New York: Harper & Brothers, 1957; Harper Torchbook, 1958), 1–4.

CHAPTER 1

1. James B. Nelson, *Embodiment: An Approach to Sexuality and Christian Theology* (Minneapolis: Augsburg, 1978), 122–23.

2. Exodus 22:21; 23:9; Deuteronomy 10:19; and Leviticus 19:33–34. See Erich Fromm, *You Shall Be As Gods: A Radical Interpretation of the Old Testament and Its Tradition* (New York: Holt, Rinehart & Winston, 1966; Henry Holt, Owl, 1991), 183–85.

3. Romans 6:1–14; 8:31–39; 1 Corinthians 15; and Philippians 2:5–8. See James M. Gustafson, *Theology and Christian Ethics* (Philadelphia: The Pilgrim Press, 1974), 136, 142–43, 158–59.

4. See Carter Heyward, *Our Passion for Justice: Images of Power, Sexuality, and Liberation* (New York: The Pilgrim Press, 1984), 83.

5. Herbert G. May and Bruce M. Metzger, eds., *The New Oxford Annotated Bible with the Apocrypha*, Revised Standard Version (New York: Oxford University Press, 1977), 149.

6. Beverly Wildung Harrison, *Making the Connections: Essays in Feminist Christian Social Ethics*, ed. Carol Rubb (Boston: Beacon Press, 1985), 129, uses this phrasing to distinguish principles from rules as resources "to open up processes of reasoning rather than close them off."

7. For an excellent reconsideration, challenge, and opening-up of the Exodus as a norm for today's social justice movements, see Robert Allen Warrior, "Canaanites, Cowboys, and Indians: Deliverance, Conquest, and Liberation Theology Today," *Christianity and Crisis*, 11 September 1989, 261–65. As a Native American, Warrior looks at the entry into (conquest of) the promised land from the viewpoint of its then current inhabitants.

8. John D'Emilio, *Sexual Politics, Sexual Communities: The Making of a Homosexual Minority in the United States, 1940–1970* (Chicago: University of Chicago Press, 1983), 69.

9. Daniel Berrigan, *No Bars to Manhood* (New York: Doubleday, 1970; Bantam, 1971), 106–18, gives an account of my trial and sentencing.

10. Fromm, *You Shall Be As Gods*, 198, in his description of the Sabbath gives me insight into the acceptance and celebration of being oneself rather than working to prove something about oneself: "'Rest' in the sense of the traditional Sabbath concept is quite different from 'rest' being defined as not working, or not making an effort. . . . On the Sabbath, [hu]man is fully [hu]man, with no task other than to be human. In the Jewish tradition it is not work which is a supreme value, but rest, the state that has no other purpose than that of being human."

11. My paraphrase of *The New Oxford Annotated Bible*, 1375.

12. Henri J. M. Nouwen, *Creative Ministry* (Garden City, N.Y.: Image Books, 1979), 17–18.

13. My paraphrase of *The New Oxford Annotated Bible*, 1227. See also Mark 9:33–37, Matthew 19:13–15, and Luke 18:15–17.

14. *The New Oxford Annotated Bible*, 836–37.

15. See Robert McAfee Brown, *Theology in a New Key: Responding to Liberation Themes* (Philadelphia: Westminster, 1978), 60–62; and Beverly Wildung Harrison, *Our Right To Choose: Toward a New Ethic of Abortion* (Boston: Beacon Press, 1983), 93.

16. Audre Lorde, *Sister Outsider: Essays and Speeches* (Trumansburg, N.Y.: Crossing, 1984), 114–15.

CHAPTER 2

1. See Paulo Freire, *Pedagogy of the Oppressed*, trans. Myra Bergman Ramos (New York: Continuum, 1985), 27–56, for a discussion of humanization and dehumanization within a social order.

2. Editors of the Harvard Law Review, *Sexual Orientation and the Law* (Cambridge, Mass.: Harvard University Press, 1990), 9–10. See also Michael Nava, "Sodomy Law Update: Repeal Efforts Should Be Given Top Priority, Say Legal Experts," *Advocate* (Los Angeles), 4 December 1990, 52–53.

3. Heyward, *Our Passion for Justice*, 75–82.

4. See, for example, Salvatore J. Licata, "The Homosexual Rights Movements in the United States," in Salvatore J. Licata and Robert P. Petersen, eds., *The Gay Past: A Collection of Historical Essays* (New York: Harrington Park, 1985), 161–89; Lillian Faderman, *Odd Girls and Twilight Lovers: A History of Lesbian Life in Twentieth Century America* (New York: Columbia University Press, 1991), 11–187; Judy Grahn, *Another Mother Tongue: Gay Words, Gay Worlds* (Boston: Beacon Press, 1984); Audre Lorde, *Zami: A New Spelling of My Name* (Freedom, Calif.: Crossing, 1982); Jonathan Katz, *Gay American History: Lesbians and Gay Men in the U.S.A.: A Documentary* (New York: Thomas Y. Crowell, 1976; Harper Colophon, 1985); Jonathan Ned Katz, *Gay/Lesbian Almanac: A New Documentary* (New York: Harper & Row, 1983); Letha Scanzoni and Virginia Ramey Mollenkott, *Is the Homosexual My Neighbor? Another Christian View* (San Francisco: Harper & Row, 1978, 1980), 32–34; Andrea Weiss and Greta Schiller, *Before Stonewall: The Making of a Gay and Lesbian Community* (Tallahassee: Naiad Press, 1988); and Quentin Crisp, *The Naked Civil Servant* (New York: Holt, Rinehart & Winston, 1968; New American Library, Plume, 1983).

5. See, for example, Douglas Crimp and Adam Rolston, *AIDS Demo Graphics* (Seattle: Bay Press, 1990).

6. For an engaging personal description and social analysis of the formation of a relationship, I recommend Barbara Macdonald and Cynthia Rich, *Look Me in the Eye: Old Women, Aging and Ageism* (San Francisco: Spinsters Ink, 1983).

7. See NYC Gay and Lesbian Anti-Violence Project, *1991 Annual Report*; "National," *Advocate* (Los Angeles), 21 April 1992, 28; "Hate Attacks Surge, Says NGLTF Report," *Task Force Report (Newsletter of the National Gay and Lesbian Task Force)*, Summer 1992, 1; and *Anti-Gay/Lesbian Violence, Victimization and Defamation in 1991* (Washington, D.C.: National Gay and Lesbian Task Force Policy Institute, 1992), for statistics on the increase in reporting of antigay/lesbian violence.

See the following articles about repeal efforts and successes in the national gay and lesbian newsmagazine *The Advocate* (Los Angeles): John Gallagher, "Colorado Measure To Bar Bias Bans Could Break Ground," 19 May 1992, 17; Brian Kelly, "Bible Thumpers Want to Repeal Rights Measure in San Diego," 8 May 1990, 20; Rick Harding, "City Council Scraps Its Own Rights Measure," 27 February 1990, 20, and "Florida Gays and Lesbians Look for

Lessons from Broward County Defeat," 9 October 1990, 19. See also Randy Shilts, *The Mayor of Castro Street: The Life and Times of Harvey Milk* (New York: St. Martin's, 1982), 212–19; Gay Rights Writer's Group, *It Could Happen to You: An Account of the Gay Civil Rights Campaign in Eugene, Oregon* (Boston: Alyson, 1983); Sarah Lyall, "Playing, and Winning, by the Rules," *New York Times*, 24 June 1992, B1, B4; and "A Blue-Collar Town Is a Gay-Rights Battleground," *New York Times*, Late Edition, 14 June 1992, 35.

See Mary B. W. Taylor, "For Gay High-School Seniors, Nightmare Is Almost Over," *New York Times*, Late Edition, 14 June 1992, 41, for a recent account of lesbian/gay high school students' experiences; and Scott A. Hunt, "An Unspoken Tragedy: Suicide Among Gay and Lesbian Youth," *Christopher Street*, 14 (1992): 28–30, for results of studies showing that "the attempted suicide rate among homosexual males is two to three times higher than the rate among heterosexual males in the same age group."

8. Sigmund Freud, *An Outline of Psycho-Analysis*, trans. James Strachey (New York: W. W. Norton, 1929), 9.

9. Ibid., 9.

10. For more extensive findings on preadolescent sexual activity, see Alfred C. Kinsey, Wardell B. Pomeroy, and Clyde E. Martin, *Sexual Behavior in the Human Male* (Philadelphia: W. B. Saunders, 1948), 157–74.

11. Noticeably absent, for example, are discussions of childhood sexuality in recent works on sexual theology and ethics, such as Nelson, *Embodiment: An Approach to Sexuality and Christian Theology* and Susan E. Davies and Eleanor H. Haney, eds., *Redefining Sexual Ethics: A Sourcebook of Essays, Stories, and Poems* (Cleveland: The Pilgrim Press, 1991). In the latter, however, Susan E. Davies' "Reflections on the Theological Roots of Abusive Behavior," 58–59, is powerful in its honest personal reflection on childhood experiences; and Sharon Hashimoto's poem, "Partings," 19–20, celebrates the physical embrace of grandmother and granddaughter, "her arms twining like leis around my neck, fingers / linked in a gentle clasp."

12. Douglas J. Besharov, *Recognizing Child Abuse: A Guide for the Concerned* (New York: Free Press, 1990), 86, reports: "The number of substantiated cases of sexual abuse rose tenfold, from about 13,000 in 1975 to over 130,000 in 1986." Studies of the law and public policy that have shaped and determined reporting practices suggest that the middle- and upper-class families are spared the kind of scrutiny that could contribute significantly to these figures; Theodore J. Stein, "The Child Abuse Prevention and Treatment Act," *Social Service Review* 58 (1984): 310, for example, observes: "The overwhelming majority of reports made by professionals (64 percent) come from persons in public sector employment. But for the schools, poor and/or

minority families are the main constituents of publicly sponsored services and are, therefore, at greatest risk of being reported. Doubtless, the public outcry would be great if reporting across social classes was significant."

13.   Marie Marshall Fortune, *Sexual Violence: The Unmentionable Sin* (New York: The Pilgrim Press, 1983), 181–83; Scanzoni and Mollenkott, *Is the Homosexual My Neighbor?*, 95–97; A. Nicholas Groth and H. Jean Birnbaum, *Men Who Rape* (New York: Plenum, 1979), 3, 148, 149; A. Nicholas Groth, "Patterns of Sexual Assault Against Children and Adolescents," in Ann Wolbert Burgess et al., *Sexual Assault of Children and Adolescents* (Lexington, Mass.: Lexington Books, 1978), 4–5; Dennis Altman, *The Homosexualization of America* (New York: St. Martin's, 1982; Boston: Beacon Press, 1983), 173, 204 n. 1; Diana Scully, *Understanding Sexual Violence: A Study of Convicted Rapists*, Perspectives on Gender, vol. 3 (Boston: Unwin Hyman, 1990), 67–70, 73; Judith Lewis Herman and Lisa Hirschman, *Father-Daughter Incest* (Cambridge: Harvard University Press, 1981), 56; and Helen Block Lewis, *Psychic War in Men and Women* (New York: New York University Press, 1976).

14.   See, for example, this description of the Mohave people by Walter L. Williams, *The Spirit and the Flesh: Sexual Diversity in American Indian Culture* (Boston: Beacon Press, 1986), 89–90: "Children spent their prepubertal years exploring their environment with their age mates, playing, swimming, indulging in sexual play and in sex itself. Because the society placed a high value on kindness of children, the Mohave child learned to like and trust everyone. Children interacted sexually and otherwise with a number of people of different ages, and did not restrict themselves to an 'overintense and exclusive emotional attachment to a single person.'"

15.   Gary Snyder, *Turtle Island* (New York: New Directions, 1974), 12–14.

16.   For an extensive discussion of mutuality between parents and children, see Christine E. Gudorf, "Parenting, Mutual Love, and Sacrifice," in Barbara Hilkert Andolsen, Christine E. Gudorf, and Mary D. Pellauer, eds., *Women's Consciousness, Women's Conscience: A Reader in Feminist Ethics* (San Francisco: Harper & Row, 1985), 175–91.

17.   Harrison, *Our Right To Choose*, 132–53.

See Kinsey et al., *Sexual Behavior in the Human Male*, 465–87, for their data on "Religious Background and Sexual Outlet." Kinsey summarizes the Jewish, Catholic, and Protestant positions on sexuality as follows:

The strictly Orthodox Jewish code and the strict Catholic interpretations differ somewhat, but both of them accept the reproductive philosophy of sex, and both of them consider sexual activities which do not offer the possibility of fruition in reproduction as morally wrong. Consequently both of them vigorously condemn masturbation, and both of them attach a tremendous importance to the value of virginity at the time of marriage. The Jewish church maintains its stand on the basis of Biblical and Talmudic interpretations. The Catholic church more often bases its interpretations on a natural philosophy which may be re-interpreted from time to time but which always emphasized the abnormality or the perverseness of sexual behavior which occurs outside of marriage.

In general, the more literal groups of the Protestant church make sexual appraisals which are close to those of the Talmud and of the Catholic natural law; but a more liberal portion of the Protestant clergy is inclined to re-interpret all types of sexual behavior in terms of the total social adjustment of the individual.

See also Robert Nugent and Jeannine Gramick, "Homosexuality: Protestant, Catholic, and Jewish Issues; A Fishbone Tale," and Yoel H. Kahn, "Judaism and Homosexuality: The Traditionalist/Progressive Debate," in Richard Hasbany, ed., *Homosexuality and Religion* (New York: Haworth, 1989), 15, 27, 33, 34, 50, 55, 71–73.

18. See Peter Brown, *The Body and Society: Men, Women, and Sexual Renunciation in Early Christianity* (New York: Columbia University Press, 1988).

19. Harrison, *Our Right To Choose*, 66.

20. John Boswell, *Christianity, Social Tolerance, and Homosexuality: Gay People in Western Europe from the Beginning of the Christian Era to the Fourteenth Century* (Chicago: University of Chicago Press, 1980), 165, citing Augustine's *De bono conjugali* 13 [15] [PL, 40:384]. See also Harrison, *Our Right To Choose*, 136–39.

21. Nelson, *Embodiment*, 53.

22. Ibid., 53–54; and Harrison, *Our Right To Choose*, 296 n. 58.

23. Harrison, *Our Right To Choose*, 65, 66–67, 142–43, 296 n. 58, 201–4.

24. Ibid., 65.

25. Colossians 3:18–25; 1 Peter 3:1–7; and Ephesians 5:21–33. See Elisabeth Schuessler Fiorenza, *In Memory of Her: A Feminist Theological Reconstruction of Christian Origins* (New York: Crossroad/Continuum, 1983), 251–84.

26. See, for example, Gerda Lerner, *The Creation of Patriarchy* (New York: Oxford University Press, 1986), 180–93; Walter Brueggemann, "The Covenanted Family: A Zone for Humanness," *Journal of Current Social Issues* 14 (1977): 18–23; Phyllis Trible, *Texts of Terror: Literary-Feminist Readings of*

Biblical Narratives, Overtures to Biblical Theology Series (Philadelphia: Fortress Press, 1984), 1–7; Fiorenza, *In Memory of Her*; Mary Daly, *The Church and the Second Sex* (New York: Harper & Row, 1968); and Carol Myers, "Gender Imagery in the Song of Songs," *Hebrew Annual Review* 10 (1986): 218.

27.   Genesis 16:1–6; 18:9–15; 24:15–25, 55–58; 27:5–17, 42–45; 29: 15–35; 30:1–24; 31:14–16, 33–35.

28.   Norman K. Gottwald, *The Hebrew Bible: A Socio-Literary Introduction* (Philadelphia: Fortress Press, 1985), 175–76.

29.   Trible, *Texts of Terror*, 1. See Genesis 16:1–16; 21:9–21; 2 Samuel 13:1–22; Judges 11: 29–40; 19:1–30.

30.   See, for example, Brueggemann, "The Covenanted Family"; and H. Eberhard von Waldow, "Social Responsibility and Social Structure in Early Israel," *Catholic Biblical Quarterly* 32 (1970): 182–204.

31.   See, for example, the discussion of the rape of Dinah (Gen. 34) by Danna Nolan Fewell and David M. Gunn, "Tipping the Balance: Sternberg's Reader and the Rape of Dinah," *Journal of Biblical Literature* 110 (1991): 193–211, especially 210–11.

32.   See, for example, Brueggemann, "The Covenanted Family."

33.   "If a man meets a virgin who is not betrothed, and seizes her and lies with her, and they are found, she shall be his wife, because he has violated her; he may not put her away all his days." Deuteronomy 22:28–29, as translated in May and Metzger, eds., *The New Oxford Annotated Bible with Apocrypha*, 243–44.

34.   Fewell and Gunn, "Tipping the Balance," 210, in their discussion of the rape of Dinah (Gen. 34), argue that the marriage offered by Shechem, Dinah's rapist, is "probably the best way for her to handle her life, given . . . the larger context of a patriarchal society": "Except to Shechem, marriage would appear to be effectively denied her. . . . In short, her best interest within the narrow limits of this society is to marry Shechem, the man who [now] loves her and takes delight in her."

35.   Lerner, *The Creation of Patriarchy*, 192–93. Some scholars argue that "the central theme of the book [of Genesis] is the assumption of paternity by males"; Sarah is mentioned later and "only as the bearer of Abraham's 'seed.'" See Lerner, 185, citing David Bakan, *And They Took Themselves Wives: The Emergence of Patriarchy in Western Civilization* (New York: Harper & Row, 1979), 27–28.

36.   For theme no. 1, see Genesis 5, 11; Numbers 1; Ruth 4:18–22; and Luke 3:23–38. For theme no. 2, see Genesis 16–17; 1 Samuel 1; and Luke 1. For theme no. 3, see Jeremiah 2:20–28; and Hosea. For theme no. 4, see Genesis 19:1–29; Leviticus 18:22, 20:13; and Romans 1:24–32.

37. See, for example, Derrick Sherwin Bailey, *Homosexuality and the Western Christian Tradition* (London: Longmans, Green, 1955); John J. McNeill, *The Church and the Homosexual* (Kansas City: Sheed Andrews and McMeel, 1976); Boswell, *Christianity, Social Tolerance, and Homosexuality*; Scanzoni and Mollenkott, *Is the Homosexual My Neighbor?*; Tom Horner, *Jonathan Loved David: Homosexuality in Biblical Times* (Philadelphia: Westminster Press, 1978); Robin Scroggs, *The New Testament and Homosexuality* (Philadelphia: Fortress Press, 1983); and George R. Edwards, *Gay/Lesbian Liberation: A Biblical Perspective* (New York: The Pilgrim Press, 1984).

38. *The New Oxford Annotated Bible*, 145, 148.

39. Congregation for the Doctrine of the Faith, "Letter to the Bishops of the Catholic Church on the Pastoral Care of Homosexual Persons," adopted in an ordinary session of the Congregation on the Doctrine of the Faith; given at Rome, 1 October 1986; approved and ordered to be published by Pope John Paul II during an audience granted to Prefect Joseph Cardinal Ratzinger; also, bearing name of Alberto Bovone, Titular Archbishop of Caesarea in Numdia, Secretary (Vatican City: Congregation for the Doctrine of Faith, 1986), 6.

40. See Mordecai Rosenfeld, "Sodom and the Constitution," *New York Law Journal*, 7 October 1986:2.

41. For a history of the portrayal of lesbian/gay people in the movies, see Vito Russo, *The Celluloid Closet: Homosexuality in the Movies* (New York: Harper & Row, 1981).

42. *The New Oxford Annotated Bible*, 22.

43. Factual evidence of imminent danger usually required by a court of law to prove that the defendant acted to prevent great bodily harm is typically not necessary in these cases. See, for example, Wainwright Churchill, *Homosexual Behavior Among Males: A Cross-Cultural and Cross-Species Investigation* (Englewood Cliffs, N.J.: Prentice-Hall, 1967; Prism, 1971), 80; Doug Ireland, "The New Homophobia: Open Season on Gays," *Nation*, 15 September 1979, 209; George Mendenhall, "Three More Killers Plead 'I Panicked': 'Homosexual Panic' Defense Spreads Around State," *Bay Area Reporter* (San Francisco), 27 October 1983, 1, 17; Lou Chibbaro, Jr., "Judge Under Fire for Remarks: Two D.C. Youths Get Probation for Brutal Attack on Gay Man," *Advocate* (Los Angeles), 10 July 1984, 16; Peter Freiberg, "Youth Acquitted in Bludgeoning Murder: Kalamazoo Gays Outraged; Judge Publicly Disagrees with Verdict," *Advocate* (Los Angeles), 1 April 1986, 12–13; Konstantin Berlandt, "100 March Against Santa Rosa Jury Verdict," *Bay Area Reporter* (San Francisco), 17 April 1983, 1, 12; Jim Ryan, "'Barbaric Behavior, Unprovoked Attack': District Gaybashers Given Light Sentences," *Washington Blade* (Washington, D.C.), 26 May 1984, 1; Arlo Smith, "Dealing with Anti-Gay Violence: 'Homosexual Panic' Defense Is Bigotry in Action," *Bay Area Reporter* (San

Francisco), 3 November 1983, 1, 11; and Robert G. Bagnall, Patrick C. Gallagher, and Joni L. Goldstein, "Burdens on Gay Litigants and Bias in the Court System: Homosexual Panic, Child Custody, and Anonymous Parties," *Harvard Civil Rights-Civil Liberties* 19 (1984): 497–559.

44.   [Jon J. Gallo, et al.], "The Consenting Adult Homosexual and the Law: An Empirical Study of Enforcement and Administration in Los Angeles County," *UCLA Law Review* 13 (1966): 644–832. See also Brian Shein, "Gay-Bashing in High Park: A Tale of Homophobia and Murder," *Toronto Life*, April 1986, 37–39, 64–69; Del Martin and Phyllis Lyon, *Lesbian/Woman* (San Francisco: Glide; revised ed., Toronto: Bantam, 1986), 45–46; Martin S. Weinberg and Collin J. Williams, *Male Homosexuals: Their Problems and Adaptations* (New York: Oxford University Press, 1974), 24–25; John Rechy, *The Sexual Outlaw: A Documentary: A Non-Fiction Account, with Commentaries, of Three Days and Nights in the Sexual Underground* (New York: Grove Press, 1977), 99; D'Emilio, *Sexual Politics, Sexual Communities*, 145–46, 183; Laud Humphreys, *Tearoom Trade: Impersonal Sex in Public Places* (Chicago: Aldine, 1970; enlarged ed., 1975), 87–90; Richard R. Troiden, "Homosexual Encounters in a Highway Rest Stop," in Erich Goode and Richard R. Troiden, eds. *Sexual Deviance and Sexual Deviants* (New York: William Morrow, 1974), 218; and Edwin M. Schur, *Crimes Without Victims: Deviant Behavior and Public Policy: Abortion, Homosexuality, Drug Addiction* (Englewood Cliffs, N.J.: Prentice-Hall, 1965), 83.

45.   May and Metzger, eds., *The New Oxford Annotated Bible with Apocrypha*, 1362.

46.   See Scroggs, *The New Testament and Homosexuality*, 59–60, 100–101, 109–18, 130–31, 140.

47.   Ibid., 101–2.

48.   Compare the other lists with the one from Romans 1 for length, content, and the parties addressed and opposed (*The New Oxford Annotated Bible*, 1362, 1376, 1384–85, 1415):

1.   Galatians 5:19–21 (to and warning "you, brethren"): "fornication, impurity, licentiousness, idolatry, sorcery, enmity, strife, jealousy, anger, selfishness, dissension, party spirit, envy, drunkenness, carousing, and the like."

2.   1 Corinthians 5:10–11 (to and about "those inside the church"): "the immoral of this world, or the greedy and robbers, or idolaters . . . guilty of immorality or greed, or is an idolater, reviler, drunkard, or robber."

3.   1 Corinthians 6:9–10 (to and about "those inside the church"): "neither the immoral, nor idolaters, nor adulterers, nor sexual

perverts, nor thieves, nor the greedy, nor drunkards, nor revilers, nor robbers."

4. 2 Corinthians 12:20 (to and about "you" in the church): "quarreling, jealousy, anger, selfishness, slander, gossip, conceit, and disorder."

5. Colossians 3:5, 8 (to "you" who "have been raised with Christ"): "fornication, impurity, passion, evil desire, and covetousness, which is idolatry. . . . anger, wrath, malice, slander, and foul talk from your mouth."

6. Romans 13:13 (to and about "ourselves"): "not in reveling and drunkenness, not in debauchery and licentiousness, not in quarreling and jealousy."

7. Romans 1:29–31 (to "you, brethren" about "them"): "filled with all manner of wickedness, evil, covetousness, malice. Full of envy, murder, strife, deceit, malignity, they are gossips, slanderers, haters of God, insolent, haughty, boastful, inventors of evil, disobedient to parents, foolish, faithless, heartless, ruthless."

In a story in the Second Book of Samuel, King David himself makes use of such a "list" of vices or misfortunes with a clear antigay slant; in a desperate attempt to discredit Joab, his errant commander in chief, he curses him as follows:

> *May the house of Joab never be without one who has a discharge, or who is leprous, or who holds a spindle, or who is slain by the sword, or who lacks bread.* (2 Samuel 3:29b; The New Oxford Annotated Bible, 379.)

On a par with serious illness, defeat in battle, and hunger is the curse of unmanliness, for "the spindle was a sign of effeminacy" (*The New Oxford Annotated Bible*, 379 n. 3.28–29). *The New American Bible* (Nashville: Thomas Nelson, 1970), 274, does not preserve the idiom and translates it as "one unmanly."

And in our own times, lesbians and gay men have all too frequently been the preferred targets of such "lists of vices" in the election bids of right-wing politicians, the immoral crusades of the religious right, and the debates about homosexuality within the range of religious denominations.

49. See Bernadette J. Brooten, "Paul's View on the Nature of Women and Female Homoeroticism," in Clarissa W. Atkinson, Constance H. Buchanan, and Margaret R. Miles, eds., *Immaculate and Powerful: The Female in Sacred Image and Social Reality* (Boston: Beacon Press, 1985), 61–87.

50. *The New Oxford Annotated Bible*, 1362.

51. Congregation for the Doctrine of the Faith, "Letter to the Bishops of the Catholic Church on the Pastoral Care of Homosexual Persons," 6.

52. Myers, "Gender Imagery in the Song of Songs," 218, writes: "The society depicted in the Bible is portrayed primarily from a male perspective, in terms of male accomplishments and in relation to a God for whom andromorphic imagery predominates. Yet in the Song, such characteristics disappear and in fact the opposite may be true; that is, a gynocentric mode predominates." Marcia Falk, *The Song of Songs: A New Translation and Interpretation* (San Francisco: Harper, 1990), 117–18, writes: "Unlike most of the Bible, the Song of Songs gives us women speaking out of their own experiences and their own imaginations, in words that do not seem filtered through the lens of patriarchal male consciousness."

53. Phyllis Trible, *God and the Rhetoric of Sexuality*, Overtures to Biblical Theology Series (Philadelphia: Fortress Press, 1978), 144–65. See also Myers, "Gender Imagery in the Song of Songs," 209–223; and Falk, *The Song of Songs*, 118, who writes: "The equally rich, sensual, emotionally expressive, and often playful language of the Song's female and male voices . . . seems to evidence a nonsexist, nonhierarchical culture—unique in the Bible. Rather than offering a reversal of stereotypical male-female relations, the Song provides a different model, one in which *all* hierarchical domination is absent. Thus the Song expresses mutuality and balance between the sexes, along with an absence of stereotyped notions of masculine and feminine behavior and characteristics."

54. Poem 6 and parts of Poems 12, 18, and 19, as divided and translated by Falk, *The Song of Songs*, 118. (Equivalent verses in *The New Oxford Annotated Bible*, 815–19, are 1:15–17; 2:16; 5:1–2,16; 6:2–3.)

55. Falk, *The Song of Songs*, 134.

56. For a history of the interpretation of the song, see H. H. Rowley, *The Servant of the Lord and Other Essays on the Old Testament* (London: Lutterworth, 1952), 189–234; and Marvin H. Pope, *The Song of Songs: A New Translation with Introduction and Commentary* (New York: Doubleday, 1977), 34–37, 40–54, 89–229.

57. May and Metzger, eds., *The New Oxford Annotated Bible*, 815.

58. Falk, *The Song of Songs*, 102, 103, 107, 113, 127, 128, says: "The Song itself never claims to be an allegory and nowhere offers an internal key to allegorical explication," as does, for example, the parable of the vineyard in Isaiah 5. To understand the form and organization of "the individual poems and of the collection as a whole," Falk, 139–61, "reveal[s] patterns in the text by illuminating settings and ambiance (which I call 'contexts'), underlying premises and ideas ('themes'), and repeated images and symbols ('motifs')." She adds that "these categories were not fixed in my mind prior to translating;

rather, they emerged during the process and, especially, afterwards, when I was able to step back from the text once again and see its contours from a new vantage point."
See also Gottwald, *The Hebrew Bible*, 547–48.
59. Michel Foucault, *The History of Sexuality*, vol. 1, *An Introduction*, trans. Robert Hurley (Paris: Editions Gallimard, 1976; New York: Pantheon, 1978; Vintage, 1980), 42–44; and Boswell, *Christianity, Social Tolerance, and Homosexuality*. See also Arthur N. Gilbert, "Conceptions of Homosexuality and Sodomy in Western History," in Licata and Petersen, eds., *The Gay Past*, 57–68.
60. For the autobiographical account of a man living in nineteenth-century United States, see Claude Hartland, *The Story of a Life: For the Consideration of the Medical Fraternity* (St. Louis, 1901; San Francisco: Grey Fox, 1985).
61. See, for example, Nancy Adair and Casey Adair, *Word Is Out: Stories of Some of Our Lives* (New York: Dell; San Francisco: New Glide, 1978); David Kopay and Perry Deane Young, *The David Kopay Story* (New York: Arbor House, 1977); Evelyn Torton Beck, ed., *Nice Jewish Girls: A Lesbian Anthology* (Trumansburg, N.Y.: Crossing, 1982); Howard Brown, *Familiar Faces, Hidden Lives: The Story of Homosexual Men in America Today* (New York: Harcourt Brace Jovanovich, 1976); Margaret Cruikshank, ed., *The Lesbian Path* (San Francisco: Grey Fox, 1980; revised and enlarged, 1985); Ruth Simpson, *From the Closet to the Courts* (New York: Viking, 1976; Penguin, 1977); Grahn, *Another Mother Tongue*; Ginny Vida, ed., *Our Right to Love: A Lesbian Resource Book* (Englewood Cliffs, N.J.: Prentice-Hall, 1978); and Martin and Lyon, *Lesbian/Woman*.
62. See Matthew 10:1–4; Mark 3:13–19; and Luke 6:12–16.
63. See Elisabeth Schuessler Fiorenza, "Discipleship and Patriarchy: Early Christian Ethos and Christian Ethics in a Feminist Theological Perspective," in Andolsen, Gudorf, Pellauer, eds., *Women's Consciousness, Women's Conscience*, 143–59.
64. Mark 3:1–6; Matthew 12:9–14; Luke 6:6–11.
65. Fromm, *You Shall Be As Gods*, 181.

Chapter 3

1. For two years I taught philosophy and religion in a maximum-security correctional facility in New York State. The courses were part of a bachelor's degree program offered in prison settings by the college at which I was also an adjunct/visiting instructor and Protestant chaplain on campus.
For comments and scholarship by women, see Elizabeth Gould Davis, *The First Sex* (Baltimore: Penguin, 1972); Daly, *The Church and the Second*

Sex; Carol P. Christ, "Why Women Need the Goddess: Phenomenological Psychological, and Political Reflection," in Carol P. Christ and Judith Plaskow, eds., *Womanspirit Rising: A Feminist Reader in Religion* (San Francisco: Harper & Row, 1979), 273–87; Merlin Stone, *When God Was a Woman* (New York: Dial Press, 1976), xv–xxvii; and Carter Heyward, *Touching Our Strength: The Erotic As Power and the Love of God* (San Francisco: Harper & Row, 1989), 84–85.

2. See Eve Kosofsky Sedgwick, *Epistemology of the Closet* (Berkeley and Los Angeles: University of California Press, 1990), 81–82.

3. Anna Quindlen, "Public and Private; Wives For Wives' Sake," *New York Times*, 9 August 1992, section 4, 17.

4. "Barbara Bush to Shun Public Stands on Issues," *New York Times*, 24 February 1989, A11. For a more recent and different incident, see also "Women's Combat Role Clarified by First Lady," *New York Times*, 20 January 1990, 12.

5. Charles Mohr, "U.S. Bans Imports of Assault Rifles in Shift by Bush," *New York Times*, 15 March 1989, A1, A25. See also Bernard Weinraub, "President Unveils $1.2 Billion Plan to Battle Crime: Ban on Rifle Is Rejected; Move on Semiautomatic Arms Is Seen as Partial Victory by Strong Gun Lobby," *New York Times*, 16 May 1989, A1, A18.

6. See Ann Petry, *Harriet Tubman, Conductor on the Underground Railroad* (New York: Pocket Books, 1971); Yisrael Gutman, *The Jews of Warsaw, 1939–1943: Ghetto, Underground, Revolt*, trans. Ina Friedman (Bloomington: Indiana University Press, 1982) (for accounts of other resistance efforts, Milton Meltzer, *Never To Forget: The Jews of the Holocaust* [New York: Harper & Row, 1976], 137–89); Jo Ann Gibson Robinson, *The Montgomery Bus Boycott and the Women Who Started It: The Memoir of Jo Ann Gibson Robinson*, ed. David J. Garrow (Knoxville: University of Tennessee Press, 1987); and Toby Marotta, *The Politics of Homosexuality* (Boston: Houghton Mifflin, 1981), 71–76.

7. Michael T. Kaufman, "Park Suspects: The Troubling Ties," *New York Times*, 26 April 1989, A1, B24.

8. Joan Morgan, "The Pro-Rape Culture: Homeboys—of All Races—Stop You in the Street," *Village Voice* (New York), 9 May 1989, 39, 52.

Chapter 4

1. *The New Oxford Annotated Bible*, 146, 147.

2. Martin Noth, *Leviticus: A Commentary*, trans. J. E. Anderson, Old Testament Library (Philadelphia: Westminster, 1965), 9–10, 136, 138–39, 146, 159, 162, 163, 165–66. See also George F. Genung, "The Book of

Leviticus," *An American Commentary on the Old Testament* (American Baptist Publication Society, 1905), v.

3. *The New Oxford Annotated Bible*, 145, 148.

4. Leviticus 20:9–16, 27; 21:9; 23:13, 16, 30; 24:17, 21. See Noth, *Leviticus*, 146–51.

5. See, for example, Rosenfeld, "Sodom and the Constitution"; and also Robert Morris, *Rethinking Social Welfare: Why Care for the Stranger?* (New York: Longman, 1986), 65–81.

6. For the term *ger*, see 16:29; 17:8, 10, 12, 13, 15; 18:26; 19:10, 33, 34(3X); 20:2; 22:18; 23:22; 24:16, 22; 25:6, 23, 45, 47(3X). See also *toshav*, which is sometimes identical in meaning to *ger*, e.g., 25:6 (verb form), 23, 35, 45 (verb form), 47(2X), and which is sometimes distinguished as less assimilated, e.g., 22:10, 40. For discussion of the term *ger*, see Noth, *Leviticus*, 131, 144; Roland de Vaux, *Ancient Israel*, vol. 1, *Social Institutions* (New York: McGraw-Hill, 1961; 1965), 74–76; Norman K. Gottwald, *The Tribes of Yahweh: A Sociology of the Religion of Liberated Israel, 1250–1050 B.C.E.* (Maryknoll, N.Y.: Orbis, 1979), 291; Mayer Sulzberger, *The Status of Labor in Ancient Israel* (Philadelphia: Dropsie College for Hebrew and Cognate Learning, 1923), 16, 21–22, 49, 51, 63–65, 86, and particularly for discussion of advance in status from earlier to later times, 25–26, 117–21; John Peter Lange, "Exodus; or, The Second Book of Moses," in *A Commentary on the Holy Scriptures*, vol. 2, trans. Charles M. Mead (New York: Scribner, Armstrong, 1876), 145; S. R. Driver, "The Book of Leviticus," *The Sacred Books of the Old and New Testaments* (New York: Dodd, Mead, 1898), 87; and A. R. S. Kennedy, *Leviticus and Numbers*, Century Bible (Edinburgh: T. C. E. and E. C. Jack [1938]), 122.

The term *rea'* occurs four times in 19:13, 16, 18; 20:10. Adjacent to and interchangeable with *rea'* is the term *'amit* (fellow, comrade), which occurs eleven times in 6:2(2X) [5:21 in Hebrew]; 19:11, 15, 17; 24:19; 25:14(2X), 15, 17, and which A. T. Chapman and A. W. Streane, *The Book of Leviticus* (Cambridge: Cambridge University Press, 1914), 139, say is an unusual Hebrew word occurring only once outside of Leviticus in Zechariah 13:7. See also Noth, *Leviticus*, 48–50, 141–42; Gordon J. Wenham, *The Book of Leviticus*, New International Commentary on the Old Testament (Grand Rapids, Mich.: William B. Eerdmans, 1979), 266–67; and Nathaniel Micklem, "The Book of Leviticus," *The Interpreter's Bible*, vol. 2 (New York: Abingdon-Cokesbury, 1953), 86.

For uses of the term *zar* and *ben-neykar*, see Leviticus 22:10, 12, 13, 25.

7. Wenham, *The Book of Leviticus*, 18. See also Noth, *Leviticus*, 16–17, 151, 160; Mary Douglas, *Purity and Danger: An Analysis of Concepts of Pollution and Taboo* (London: Routledge and Kegan Paul, 1966, 1979), 49–51; Robert North, *Sociology of the Biblical Jubilee*, Analecta Biblica Investigationes Sci-

entificae in Res Biblicas 4 (Rome: Pontifical Biblical Institute, 1954), 222–23; S. H. Kellogg, *The Book of Leviticus*, Expositor's Bible (London: Hodder and Stoughton, 1891), 503; James L. Mays, *Leviticus, Numbers*, Layman's Bible Commentaries (London: SCM, 1963), 55–66; Micklem, "The Book of Leviticus," 87, 88; and Kennedy, *Leviticus and Numbers*, 124–25.

8. In this passage the term *bdl*, meaning "to distinguish or separate," occurs four times as well. See its use also in Leviticus 10:10 and 11:47. See also the term *nazer*, "to separate, restrain, or dedicate," in 15:31 and 22:2, and *cherem*, "devoted" or "most holy," in 27:28.

9. *The New Oxford Annotated Bible*, 148.

10. For references to "cutting off," see Leviticus 7:20, 21, 25, 27; 17:4, 9, 10, 14; 18:29; 20:3, 5, 6, 17, 18; 23:29, 30. See also Micklem, "The Book of Leviticus," 37–38; and Wenham, *The Book of Leviticus*, 233, 241–42, 285–86.

For other references to keeping separate from other nations, see 18:24, 28; 20:23; 25:44; 26:33, 38, 45.

For discussion and commentary on "cleanness" regulations, see Noth, *Leviticus*, 89–126; Wenham, *The Book of Leviticus*, 161–238; Gottwald, *The Hebrew Bible*, 473–77; Mays, *Leviticus, Numbers*, 44–54; and Douglas, *Purity and Danger*, 41–57.

A theme of "inside/outside," in which inside is good or holy and outside is bad or unholy, runs through Leviticus. For example: "outside the camp" (4:11–12, 21; 6:11; 8:17; 9:11; 16:27; 10:4–5; 13:46; 14:3; 24:14, 23); "into the camp" (14:8; 16:26, 28); "not to go out of sanctuary" (21:12); "outside of the city" (14:40, 41, 45, 53); "into the holy place" versus "into the wilderness" (16:2–3, 20–22); "vomit/cast out of the land those who defile themselves" (18:24–25, 28; 20:22, 23); "into the land of Canaan" (14:34; 18:3; 20:22; 23:10; 25:2); "out of the land of Egypt" (11:45; 18:3); "come into, bring to, or bring before the tent of the meeting" (4:4, 5, 14, 16; 9:23; 10:9; 16:23; 17:5; 19:21); "not bringing to door of the tent of meeting" (17:4, 9); "not to go out from door of the tent of the meeting" (10:7); "draw near" (9:5, 7, 8; 10:3, 4, 5; 16:1; 21:18, 21, 23); "bring within the veil" (16:2, 12, 15; 21:23). See Micklem, "The Book of Leviticus," 119, who writes about 24:14, 23: "'The whole ceremony is purgative, not judicial,' i.e., the thought underlying it is not the fitting of the penalty to the crime but the removal, as it were, of a spot of infection from the community."

11. See Noth, *Leviticus*, 56–57, 153–163; Martin Noth, *The Old Testament World*, trans. Victor I. Gruhn (Philadelphia: Fortress Press, 1960), 168; and Leviticus 6:18, 29; 7:6; 21:7, 9, 13–15, 18–24; 22:12–13.

12. See Leviticus 1:3, 10; 4:3, 23, 28; 5:15, 18; 6:6; 12:1–5; 27:1–7. See Noth, *Leviticus*, 97, 204–5; Kennedy, *Leviticus and Numbers*, 177; and Chapman and Streane, *The Book of Leviticus*, 176.

13. See Leviticus 18:6–18; 20:10–12. See also Herman and Hirschman, *Father-Daughter Incest*, 61.

14. *The New Oxford Annotated Bible*, 97, 154.

15. Ibid., 154.

16. North, *Sociology of the Biblical Jubilee*, 45, 114, 143–47, 155–58, 165–67, 173, 175, 215; and Noth, *Leviticus*, 140, 183–89. The jubilee law was to "to be in force for all the 'inhabitants' of the land [25:10], meaning here in a precise sense all those who were settled on and had a stake in the land, in practice the heads of families" (Noth, *Leviticus*, 187). A family as described by Leviticus consisted of a wife, children, hired servants, and slaves headed by a property-owning man (18:6–16; 20:10–12, 17–21; 25:10, 44–46). See also Genung, "The Book of Leviticus," xiii; Micklem, "The Book of Leviticus," 37–38, 129.

Biblical passages are quoted from *The New Oxford Annotated Bible*, 97, 154.

For comparison of Exodus 23:10–11 and Leviticus 25:1–7, see Noth, *Leviticus*, 185–89; and Kennedy, *The Book of Leviticus*, 172. See H. Eberhard von Waldow, "Social Responsibility and Social Structure in Early Israel," *Catholic Biblical Quarterly* 32 (1970): 182–204, who cites the three-membered formula of sojourner-widow-orphan in Deuteronomy 10:18; 16:11, 14; 24:19–21; Jeremiah 7:6; 22:3; Ezekiel 22:7; Psalm 94:6; 146:9.

Provisions for feeding the poor (*ani*) are mentioned in Leviticus only in 19:10 and 23:22, but widows and orphans are not mentioned specifically. See Mays, *Leviticus, Numbers*, 59; and Genung, "The Book of Leviticus," 80.

Allowances for those "who cannot afford" to participate in cultic practices are prescribed in Leviticus 5:7–13; 12:8; 14:21–32; and 27:8.

See John Hart, *The Spirit of the Earth: A Theology of the Land* (New York: Paulist, 1984), 74–77, for a social justice application of the Jubilee Year.

17. For discussion of the fall of Jerusalem and Cyrus's decree, see Martin Noth, *The History of Israel* (New York: Harper & Row, 1958; 2d ed., 1960), 280–356.

18. See Gottwald, *The Hebrew Bible*, 202–3, 207, 414, 433; Noth, *Leviticus*, 10–15, 129–30; Chapman and Streane, *The Book of Leviticus*, xi–xiii, 136, 156–73; and Martin Noth, *A History of Pentateuchal Traditions*, trans. Bernhard W. Anderson (Englewood Cliffs, N.J.: Prentice Hall, 1972), 8–9, 46–62, 271–72; Noth, *Leviticus*, 10–15; Kennedy, *Leviticus and Numbers*, 20–31; and Driver, "The Book of Leviticus," 56–58.

19. Gottwald, *The Hebrew Bible*, 423. See also 424–25, 428–29, 432, 437, 460–62, 491; and Noth, *The History of Israel*, 282–96, 302–7, 314–15, 317–18, 322–23, 330, 333, 338–39.

20.   Gottwald, *The Hebrew Bible*, 413, 473. See also Noth, *The History of Israel*, 297, 330, 314–16, 333, 336–37; Noth, *Leviticus*, 129–30, 165–66, 176–77, 185, 200–201; Gottwald, *The Hebrew Bible*, 423–32, 437, 460–63; and North, *Sociology of the Biblical Jubilee*, 143–44, 158, 222–23.

21.   Compare Exodus 20:14; 22:16, 19 (with death prescribed once and only for bestiality), Deuteronomy 22:13–30; 27:20–23 (with death prescribed three times for deception by a virgin, adultery, adultery with a virgin), and Leviticus 18:6–20, 22–23; 20:10–21 (with death prescribed seven times and being "cut off from their people" twice for various forms of adultery and incest, male homosexuality, marrying a daughter and her mother, bestiality, and having sex with a menstruating woman).

22.   The term "I am Yahweh" appears twice in Exodus 20:2, 5 and twice in Deuteronomy 5:6, 9. Within Leviticus it appears fifty-two times, half of them in chapters 18, 19, and 20.

See Kennedy, *Leviticus and Numbers*, 124–25; Chapman and Streane, *The Book of Leviticus*, xlviii; Micklem, "The Book of Leviticus," 86; and Wenham, *The Book of Leviticus*, 250–51.

23.   Gottwald, *The Hebrew Bible*, 491.

24.   Benjamin Friedman, *Day of Reckoning: The Consequences of American Economic Policy Under Reagan and After* (New York: Random House, 1988), 20, 50, 90–91.

25.   Ibid., 39–44, 97.

26.   Doug Henwood, "American Dream: It's Not Working," *Christianity and Crisis*, 8 June 1992, 195, 196.

27.   Ibid., 195.

28.   Friedman, *Day of Reckoning*, 39–44, 97. See Gordon Allport, *The Nature of Prejudice* (Chicago: Addison-Wesley, 1954).

29.   Henwood, "American Dream," 195–96.

30.   Friedman, *Day of Reckoning*, 39–44, 97. See Allport, *The Nature of Prejudice*.

31.   Henwood, "American Dream," 195.

32.   William Tabb, "Competition: The Reich Recipe," *Christianity and Crisis*, 8 June 1992, 204.

33.   Theodore J. Stein, *Child Welfare and the Law* (New York: Longman, 1991), 5–6, 89.

34.   Nugent and Gramick, "Homosexuality"; Kahn, "Judaism and Homosexuality"; and Aaron Cooper, "No Longer Invisible: Gay and Lesbian Jews Build a Movement," in Richard Hasbany, ed., *Homosexuality and Religion*, 15, 16, 19, 21, 57, 58–59, 84–84.

See R. W. Weltge, *The Same Sex: An Appraisal of Homosexuality* (Philadelphia: The Pilgrim Press, 1969); "Historic Ordination 20 Years Ago,"

United Church News, June 1992, 3; J. M. Saslow, "Hear O Israel," *Advocate* (Los Angeles), 3 February 1987, 38–41, 44–48, 108–11; John McNeill, "The Christian Male Homosexual," *Homiletic and Pastoral Review* 70 (1970): 667–77, 747–58, 828–36; Salvatorian Gay Ministry Task Force, *Ministry/USA: A Model for Ministry to the Homosexual Community* (Milwaukee: National Center for Gay Ministry, 1974).

35. See Linda Greenhouse, "The Court's Shift to the Right," *New York Times*, 7 June 1989, A1, A22; Charles Stephen Ralston, "Court vs. Congress: Judicial Interpretation of The Civil Rights Acts and Congressional Response," *Yale Law & Policy Review* 8 (1990): 205–22; and Stephen Reinhardt, "The Trickle Down of Judicial Racism [Speech]," *Harper's*, August 1992, 15–17.

36. *Alyeska Pipeline Service Co. v. Wilderness Society* (1975), *General Electric Co. v. Gilbert* (1976), *City of Mobile v. Bolden* (1980), and *Grove City College v. Bell* (1984). See Ralston, "Court vs. Congress: Judicial Interpretation of The Civil Rights Acts and Congressional Response," *Yale Law & Policy Review* 8 (1990): 209–10.

37. Ralston, "Court vs. Congress," 205, 211–16. All in 1989: *Price Waterhouse v. Hopkins*, *Wards Cove Packing Co. v. Antonio*, *Martin v. Wilks*, *Lorance v. AT&T Technologies*, *Patterson v. MacLean Credit Union*, *Jett v. Dallas Indep[endent] School District*, and *Independent Fed[eratio]'n of Flight Attendants v. Zipes*.

38. See Stein, *Child Welfare and the Law*, 6; Arthur S. Leonard, "Getting Beyond *Hardwick*," *New York Native*, 1 September 1986, 20; and Linda Vance, "Gay Sex in the Sights of the Right: Intimate Inequality in the Minds of the Supreme Court," *Gay Community News* (Boston), Summer 1986.

39. For example, *Harris v. McRae* (1980); *H. L. v. Matheson* (1981); *Webster v. Reproductive Health Services* (1989); *Rust v. Sullivan* (1991); and *Planned Parenthood v. Casey* (1992). See "Over 16 Years, High Court Has Shaped Abortion Policy," *New York Times*, 4 July 1989; and Kathleen M. Sullivan, "A Victory for Roe," *New York Times*, 30 June 1992, A23.

40. For tally of vote in the House, see Mary Frances Berry, *Why ERA Failed: Politics, Women's Rights, and the Amending Process of the Constitution* (Bloomington: Indiana University Press, 1986), 106. See also 101–20; Jane J. Mansbridge, *Why We Lost the ERA* (Chicago: University of Chicago Press, 1986); and Beverly Harrison, "The Equal Rights Amendment: A Moral Analysis," in *Making the Connections*, ed. Carol S. Robb, 167–73.

41. See Arthur S. Leonard, "Gay and Lesbian Rights Protection in the U.S.: An Introduction to Gay and Lesbian Civil Rights" (Washington, D.C.: National Gay and Lesbian Task Force, [1989]); Shilts, *The Mayor of Castro Street*, 212–19; Gay Rights Writer's Group, *It Could Happen to You*; Sarah Lyall, "Playing, and Winning, by the Rules," *New York Times*, 24 June 1992, B1, B4; and National Gay and Lesbian Task Force, *Summary of Civil Rights*

Laws which Include Sexual Orientation (Washington, D.C.: National Gay and Lesbian Task Force, September 1992).

For a sample of various actions prompted by proposed lesbian/gay rights legislation, see the following articles published in the national gay and lesbian newsmagazine, the *Advocate* (Los Angeles): (1) by Chris Bull, "Rights Bill Looks Secure: Massachusetts Measure Is Saved by Religion," 30 January 1990, 13; "Vermont Lawmakers Approve Bias Ban; Enactment Is Likely," 19 May 1992, 17; "Phoenix Approves Limited Bias Ban, Eyes Bigger Prize," 28 January 1992, 17; (2) by Brian Kelly, "Bible Thumpers Want to Repeal Rights Measure in San Diego," 8 May 1990, 20; (3) by John Gallagher, "The Right's New Strategy," 30 July 1992, 46–49; "Colorado Measure To Bar Bias Bans Could Break Ground," 19 May 1992, 14–15; "Language Gets Rough as Colorado Cities Debate Rights Laws," 9 April 1991, 25; "Quiet Lobbying Work Wins Hawaii a Law Forbidding Job Bias," 23 April 1991, 29; and (4) by Rick Harding, "City Council Scraps Its Own Rights Measure," 27 February 1990, 20; "Despite Gays' Court Win, Massachusetts's Rights Law Remains Imperiled," 14 August 1990, 17; "Florida Gays and Lesbians Look for Lessons from Broward County Defeat," 9 October 1990, 19; "Outlook Called Rosy for Gay Rights Bill in Connecticut," 29 January 1991, 19.

42. "Civil Rights Shocker," *Task Force Report (Newsletter of the National Gay and Lesbian Task Force*, Summer 1992, 2. See also Timothy Egan, "Oregon Measure Asks State to Repress Homosexuality," *New York Times*, section 1, pp. 1, 34.

43. Lyall, "Playing, and Winning, by the Rules," B1, B4; Jane Gross, "In Reversal, California Governor Signs a Bill Extending Gay Rights," *New York Times*, 26 September 1992, 1, 8; Jeffrey Schmalz, "Gay Areas Are Jubilant Over Clinton: Oregon Defeats Bid to Curb Gay Rights," *New York Times*, 5 November 1992, B7.

44. Nugent and Gramick, "Homosexuality," and Kahn, "Judaism and Homosexuality," in Hasbany, ed., *Homosexuality and Religion*, 22–28, 60–65.

See Ari L. Goldman, "Highest Presbyterian Panel Bars Homosexual Minister," *New York Times*, 5 November 1992, B21; Peter Steinfels, "Vatican Condones Some Discrimination Against Homosexuals," *New York Times*, 18 July 1992, 7; Jim Gittings, "Clergy and Sexuality: The Pot Still Simmers," *Christianity and Crisis*, 20 July 1992, 250–51; Chris Bull, "Rights Issues Get Attention from Baptists," *Advocate* (Los Angeles), 7 April 1992, 20; John Gallagher, "Pastor's Selection Sparks New Uproar for Presbyterians," *Advocate* (Los Angeles), 11 February 1992, 15; "Kinnamon Loses," *United Church News*, November 1991, 11; Rob Gascho, "The Journey Is Our Home: A Brief History of BMC," *Dialogue* (Newsletter of Brethren/Mennonite Council for Lesbian and Gay Concerns), March 1991, 1–2; Peter Steinfels, "Alter Law on Sex, Panel Asks Church: Presbyterians Urged to Ordain Gay Ministers—

Intense Dissension Is Expected," *New York Times*, 1 March 1991, A20; Rick Harding, "Methodists Clash Over Gay Marriage," *Advocate* (Los Angeles), 19 June 1990, 13; Nancy Hardesty, "Holy Wars: Gays and Lesbians Fight Organized Religion," *Advocate* (Los Angeles), 4 December 1990, 34–35; Wickie Stamps, "No Church Lady: How Minister Rose Mary Denman Lost a Trial and Won a New Life," *Advocate* (Los Angeles), 4 December 1990, 40; Rose Mary Denman, "Looking Forward, Looking Back," *Christianity and Crisis*, 1 February 1988, 7–8; Peter Steinfels, "Methodists Vote to Retain Policy Condemning Homosexual Behavior," *New York Times*, A22; David Perry, "Lutheran Seminarians Face 'New Inquisition,'" *Advocate* (Los Angeles), 5 July 1988, 37–39; Zalmon O. Sherwood, *Kairos: Confessions of a Gay Priest* (Boston: Alyson, 1987); James L. Franklin, "Methodist Minister Faces Dismissal as Lesbian," *Boston Globe*, 19 May 1987; Joan L. Clark, "Coming Out: The Process and Its Price," *Christianity and Crisis*, 11 June 1979, 146–53.

For information about problems within gay/lesbian-positive denominations, see Bill Meunier, "Brown Deer Church Parishoners Vote to Retain Lesbian Minister," *Wisconsin Light* (Madison), 1 May 1991, 1, 7; F. Jay Deacon, "'Common Vision' Survey Finds Mixed Views of Gay/Lesbian Inclusion in Unitarian Universalism," *Ethics & Actions* (Department for Social Justice, Unitarian Universalist Association), June 1988, 1, 3, 18; W. Evan Golder, "Homosexual Candidates for Ministry Challenge UCC Ordination Polity," *United Church News*, February 1988, 8; Peter Freiberg, "Congregation Ousts Mich. Gay Priest," *Advocate* (Los Angeles), 22 December 1987, 16–17; Gary David Comstock, "Aliens in the Promised Land?" *USQR: Union Seminary Quarterly Review* 41 (1987): 93–104; and Gerald Renner, "Homosexuals Find Doors to Ordination Tightly Closed," *Hartford Courant* (Hartford, Conn.), 27 January 1986, A1, A10.

45.   See, for example, Altman, *The Homosexualization of America*, 128–31.

46.   Nava, "Sodomy Law Update," 53.

47.   Gallup polls frequently reported on television show that over the past several years (1988–1992) the approval ratings have remained constant: 26 percent of the adult population want abortion to be made illegal; 53 percent favor some restrictions; and 33 percent want full legality. See Sullivan, "A Victory for Roe," *New York Times*, 30 June 1992, A23.

See "Homosexuals in America," *The Gallup Opinion Index: Political, Social and Economic Trends* 147 (October 1977): 1; Gary David Comstock, *Violence Against Lesbians and Gay Men* (New York: Columbia University Press, 1991), 168; Bull, "Rights Bill Looks Secure," 13; Altman, *The Homosexualization of America*, 101–2; Jeannine Gramick, "Homosexuality to Be a Burning Catholic Issue" [Letter], *New York Times*, 11 July 1992, 18; Steinfels, "Vatican Condones Some Discrimination Against Homosexuals," *New York Times*, 18 July

1992, 7. Gallup reports in a June 1977 poll that 56 percent of Americans favored equal employment opportunities for lesbians and gay men, and in a May 1992 poll that 78 percent of American Catholics support such equal employment rights. My survey of college students found that eighty-one of the respondents support lesbian/gay rights (45 percent for full equality; 36 percent for rights in some areas). Bull reports that polls in Massachusetts found that "70% of respondents said they support the state gay rights bill." Gramick reports that in the past five years there has been a 20 percent decrease in the number of Catholics who agree with the church's teaching on same-sex behavior.

48. Mansbridge, *Why We Lost the ERA*, 201–18. See also Harrison, *Making the Connections*, 170–71.

49. Noth, *A History of Pentateuchal Traditions*, 47–62. See Michael Walzer, *Exodus and Revolution* (New York: Basic Books, 1985).

50. See Martin Noth, *Exodus: A Commentary*, trans. J. S. Bowden, Old Testament Library (Philadelphia: Westminster, 1962), 9–17.

51. *The New Oxford Annotated Bible*, 69–70.

52. Noth, *A History of Pentateuchal Traditions*, 47–62.

53. Audre Lorde, "Age, Race, Class, and Sex: Women Redefining Difference," in *Sister Outsider*, 114, 115, 123.

54. Audre Lorde, "There Is No Hierarchy of Oppressions," *Interracial Books for Children Bulletin* 14, nos. 3, 4 (1983): 9.

CHAPTER 5

1. In 1 Samuel Jonathan makes six appearances: in chapter 13 he strikes down the pillar of the Philistines at Geba; in chapter 14 he is a heroic warrior at Michmash; in chapter 18 he makes a covenant with David; in chapter 19 he warns David of Saul's anger; in chapter 20 he advises David to flee from Saul; and in chapter 23 he goes to and comforts David in the wilderness. Also, in chapter 22, in conversation with his servants, Saul refers to "my son" as making "a league with [David], the son of Jesse . . . against me"; and in chapter 31 Jonathan is mentioned as dying alongside Saul and his two other sons in the battle of Gilboa.

In 2 Samuel a messenger announces and David laments Jonathan's death in chapter 1; Jonathan's son, Meribbaal, is introduced in chapter 4 as having fled and become crippled after the defeat of Saul; David welcomes Meribbaal into his house in chapter 9; the servant of Meribbaal betrays his master's loyalty to David in chapter 16; Meribbaal demonstrates his loyalty to David in chapter 19; and David spares the life of Meribbaal and recovers and buries the bones of Saul and Jonathan in chapter 21.

2. Abridged from *The New Oxford Annotated Bible*, 346–50, 353–60, 363, 373–75, 386, 396, 402, 405–6.

3. Johs. Pedersen, *Israel: Its Life and Culture*, vols. 1–2 (London: Oxford University Press, 1926; reprinted, 1954), 25. See also A. F. Kirkpatrick, *The First and Second Books of Samuel* (London: Cambridge University Press, 1889; revised, 1930), 436; and W. O. E. Oesterley, *The First Book of Samuel* (London: Cambridge University Press, 1913), 60.

4. See Kirkpatrick, *The First and Second Books of Samuel*, liii; Hans Wilhelm Hertzberg, *I and II Samuel: A Commentary*, trans. J. S. Bowden (Philadelphia: Westminster, 1964), 111, 115, 132; Oesterley, *The First Book of Samuel*, 71–72; Julius Wellhausen, *Prolegomena to the History of Israel*, trans. J. Sutherland Black and Allan Menzies (Edinburgh: Adam and Charles Black, 1895), 450; P. Kyle McCarter, Jr., *I Samuel: A New Translation with Introduction, Notes, and Commentary* (Garden City, N.Y.: Doubleday, 1980), 251; S. R. Driver, *Notes on the Hebrew Text and the Topography of the Books of Samuel with an Introduction in Hebrew Palaeography and the Ancient Versions* (Oxford: Clarendon, 1913), 114–15; Joseph Blenkinsopp, "Jonathan's Sacrilege: I SM 14, 1–46: A Study in Literary History," *Catholic Biblical Quarterly* 26 (1964): 444–45; and Bruce C. Birch, *The Rise of the Israelite Monarchy: The Growth and Development of I Samuel 7–15*, Society of Biblical Literature Dissertation Series 27 (Missoula, Mont.: Scholars Press, 1976), 125 n. 151.

5. Kirkpatrick, *The First and Second Books of Samuel*, liii. Blenkinsopp, "Jonathan's Sacrilege," 444–45, observes that "I SM 14 is an incident in the Philistine war, a war which must be considered a bridge between the old order or a loose tribal confederation and the new ostensibly secular reality of the monarchy."

6. McCarter, *I Samuel: A New Translation*, 248–51, says: (1) that "nowhere in the OT is such detail given concerning casting lots," and (2) that the prophetic author of 1 Samuel 13:7b–15a selected the accounts of the battle of Michmash Pass and the cursing of Jonathan because they showed what the author believed to be true about Saul, i.e., that he tried to manipulate the divine will through ritual formality. See also Peter R. Ackroyd, *The First Book of Samuel* (London: Cambridge University Press, 1971), 112–14; and Kirkpatrick, *The First and Second Books of Samuel*, 96.

7. 1 Samuel 14:45. See David Jobling, "Saul's Fall and Jonathan's Rise: Tradition and Redaction in 1 Sam. 14:1–46," *Journal of Biblical Literature* 95 (1976): 367–76.

8. Hertzberg, *I and II Samuel: A Commentary*, 244.

9. See J. A. Thompson, *The Ancient Near Eastern Treaties and the Old Testament* (London: Tyndale, 1963); and George E. Mendenhall, *Law and Covenant in Israel and the Ancient Near East* (Pittsburgh: Biblical Colloquium, 1955).

10.   J. A. Thompson, "The Significance of the Verb Love in the David-Jonathan Narratives in 1 Samuel," Vetus Testamentum 24 (1974): 336–37.

11.   William L. Moran, "The Ancient Near Eastern Background of the Love of God in Deuteronomy," Catholic Biblical Quarterly 25 (1963): 80.

12.   See Encyclopedia of Religion, s.v. "Covenant," by Delbert R. Hillers; Interpreter's Dictionary of the Bible, s.v. "Covenant," by G. E. Mendenhall; Encyclopedia of Christianity, s.v. "Covenants, Biblical," by Harry Buis; and Encyclopaedia of Religion and Ethics, s.v. "Covenant," by John Herkless.

13.   Interpreter's Dictionary of the Bible, s.v. "Covenant," by Mendenhall.

14.   See Gottwald, The Hebrew Bible, 315; David M. Gunn, The Fate of King Saul: An Interpretation of a Biblical Story (Sheffield: JSOT, 1980), 14, 80, 81, 84, 93, 120; Ackroyd, The First Book of Samuel, 147, 167; and David Jobling, The Sense of Biblical Narrative: Three Structural Analyses in the Old Testament (1 Samuel 13–31, Numbers 11–12, 1 Kings 17–18) (Sheffield: JSOT, 1978), 13–14.

15.   1 Samuel 13:13–14; 15:11–35.

16.   Such is the case with the other covenants not related to Jonathan and David in 1 and 2 Samuel, as well as with the well-known covenants elsewhere in the Old Testament that God made with Noah, Abraham, and Moses: 1 Samuel 11:1–2; 2 Samuel 3:12–13, 21; 5:3; 23:5; Genesis 9:8–12; 17:1–14; and Exodus 24:8.

17.   Biblical scholars have noted that conventional covenant-making formula and terminology are altered here. See Driver, Notes on the Hebrew Text and the Topography of the Books of Samuel, 149; and Walter Harrelson, Interpreting the Old Testament (New York: Holt, Rinehart & Winston, 1964), 168.

18.   Harrelson, Interpreting the Old Testament, 168.

19.   1 Samuel 23:18. The only other covenant-making between equals that I know of in the Old Testament is between Jacob and Laban in Genesis 31:44.

20.   1 Samuel 20:8–23, 42; 23:16–18; and 2 Samuel 9:1–8.

21.   1 Samuel 18:3; 20:42.

22.   See William McKane, I and II Samuel: Introduction and Commentary (London: SCM, 1963), 137; and A. R. S. Kennedy, Samuel, The New Century Bible (Edinburgh: T. C. and E. C. Jack, [n.d.]; New York: Henry Frowde, n.d.), 151.

23.   Gunn, The Fate of King Saul, 84.

24.   Jobling, The Sense of Biblical Narrative, 20.

25.   Joseph Cady, "'Drum-Taps' and Nineteenth-Century Male Homosexual Literature," in Walt Whitman: Here and Now, ed. J. P. Krieg (Westport, Conn.: Greenwood, 1985), 52.

See also Lillian Faderman, *Surpassing the Love of Men* (New York: William Morrow, 1981), 400–405, for decoding of Gertrude Stein's writing.

26.   Cady, "'Drum-Taps' and Nineteenth-Century Male Homosexual Literature," 53.

27.   A measure of the success of such coding may be the clarity with which gay persons today tend to read the David-Jonathan relationship as romantic and nongay persons read it as political or friendly. Compare, for example, Horner, *Jonathan Loved David*, and Boswell, *Christianity, Social Tolerance, and Homosexuality*, 238–39, 252, with Gerald T. Sheppard, "The Use of Scripture within the Christian Ethical Debate Concerning Same-Sex Oriented Persons," *USQR* 40 (1985): 21, 34 n. 27; Bailey, *Homosexuality and the Western Christian Tradition*, 56–57; Kirkpatrick, *The First and Second Books of Samuel*, 152; and *The Universal Jewish Encyclopedia* 6.180. However, note the omission or avoidance of any discussion of Jonathan and David's relationship by nongay scholar George R. Edwards, *Gay/Lesbian Liberation*, and by gay scholar John J. McNeill, *The Church and the Homosexual*.

28.   See, for example, Tennyson's *In Memoriam* and Walt Whitman, "Vigil Strange I Kept on the Field One Night" from "Drum-Taps," in *Leaves of Grass* (New York: New American Library, Signet Classic, 1980), 249.

29.   See Song of Solomon 1:16 and Psalm 133:1.

Perhaps, though, the coding was not subtle enough, since the Vulgate has: "As a mother loveth her only son, so did I love thee" (Kirkpatrick, *The First and Second Books of Samuel*, 250).

Problems that have occurred traditionally in translating certain words, such as "bow" in 2 Samuel 1:18 and "thy glory" or "gazelle" in 2 Samuel 1:19, may for a gay man present clear signals and less of an obstacle. The "bow" could refer quite easily to Jonathan, since the bow was a gift of their covenant (1 Sam. 18:4) and bow-and-arrow shooting was the activity around which one of their farewell meetings occurred (1 Sam. 20:35–42). The possible double meaning of "thy glory" or "gazelle" lets a gay man favor the latter to refer to and remember the Jonathan who swiftly crossed mountain ranges to visit David in his time of need (1 Sam. 23:15–18). Such a coded introductory reference—along with the concluding reference to David's love for Jonathan (2 Sam. 1:26)—allows for a camouflaged framing of the entire lament in favor of Jonathan while preserving the explicitly balanced homage to Saul and Jonathan.

30.   I find encouragement in Adrienne Rich's advice about recovering and reclaiming our pasts: "We need a lot more documentation about what actually happened. I think we can also imagine it, because we know it happened—we know it out of our own lives" (Adrienne Rich, in Elly Bulkin, "An Interview with Adrienne Rich: Part I," *Conditions: One*, 1977, 62).

31. See Derek Cohen and Richard Dyer, "The Politics of Gay Culture," in Gay Left Collective, *Homosexuality: Power and Politics* (London: Allison & Busby, 1980), 172; and Altman, *The Homosexualization of America*, 155–57.

32. *The New Oxford Annotated Bible*, 332.

CHAPTER 6

1. See Sheila D. Collins, "The Familial Economy of God," *Theology in the Americas Documentation Series* no. 8 (New York: Theology of the Americas, 1979).

2. See Matthew 10:34.

3. See Matthew 11:25–27; Luke 22:28–30; John 3:34–36; 14:1–31; 17:1–26; and also the popular hymn "Christ the Lord Is Risen Today" (lyrics by Charles Wesley, 1707–1788; music *Lyra Davidica*, 1708), especially the opening of the second stanza, "Lives again our glorious king."

4. See Matthew 6:25–34; Mark 6:30–56; and Luke 12:22–34.

5. See Luke 6:20–42 and 12:54–59.

6. See Mark 9:35–37; Luke 24:28–30; and John 16:16–28.

7. See Matthew 9:9–10 and Luke 18:9–14.

8. See Matthew 9:18–26; Mark 5:21–24, 35–43; Luke 8:40–42, 49–56; and John 3:1–14.

9. See John 4:46–53.

10. Matthew 8:5–13; Luke 7:1–10. *The New Oxford Annotated Bible*, 1180, 1252.

11. See Matthew 26:6–13; Mark 14:3–9; and John 12:1–8.

12. Matthew 26:6–11. Mark 14:5 and John 12:5 emphasize the costliness of the ointment by adding that it could have been sold "for more than three hundred denarii" or "for three hundred denarii"; a denarius was a day's wage for a laborer (*The New Oxford Annotated Bible*, 1207, 1234, 1305).

13. John 8:2–11.

14. Even within liberal denominations, like my own, a question asked of candidates for membership within a local congregation is, "Do you profess Jesus Christ as Lord and Savior?" *Book of Worship: United Church of Christ* (New York: United Church of Christ, Office for Church Life and Leadership, 1986), 161.

15. Elie Wiesel, *A Jew Today*, trans. Marion Wiesel (New York: Random House, 1978; Vintage, 1979), 17–23. See also Elie Wiesel, *Night*, trans. Stella Rodway (Paris: Editions de Minuit, 1958; New York: Bantam, 1982).

16. Lorde, *Sister Outsider*, 110–13.

17. John 13:13–16a, 33–35; 15:12–17 (my paraphrase of *The New Oxford Annotated Bible*, 1307, 1308, 1310).

18. A notable exception may be the major role that churches have played in initiating and providing day-care programs for children. See Eileen W. Lindner, Mary C. Mattis, and June R. Rogers, *When Churches Mind the Children: A Study of Day Care in Local Parishes* (Ypsilanti, Mich.: High/Scope, 1983).

19. Martin Luther King, Jr., *Why We Can't Wait* (New York: Harper & Row, 1963; New American Library, Mentor, 1964), 76–95.

20. Reinhold Niebuhr, *Leaves from the Notebook of a Tamed Cynic* (Chicago: Willett, Clark and Colby, 1929), 69.

21. Lorde, *Sister Outsider*, 110–13.

22. I conducted these surveys in the summers of 1990 and 1991. Two-hundred-eighty-nine people responded from the United Church of Christ (UCC) and 189 from the United Methodist Church (UMC). Seventy-four percent of the UCC respondents and 78 percent of the UMC respondents report involvement in what they consider to be ministry outside of their respective denominations. The most frequently reported forms of ministry from the combined samples were AIDS advocacy and services (42%), volunteer counseling (34%), lesbian/gay support and activism (21%), hunger projects (15%), homeless projects (15%), community services (13%), social justice advocacy (12%), interfaith events and organizations (11%), women's antiviolence projects (10%), and youth programs (7%).

23. Snyder, *Turtle Island*.

24. Genesis 12:1–10 (my paraphrase of *The New Oxford Annotated Bible*, 14–15).

25. George Jackson, *Soledad Brother: The Prison Letters of George Jackson* (New York: Bantam, 1970); quoted in a paper written by a student for a course titled "Religion and Human Development," which I taught at Green Haven Correctional Facility in the summer of 1989.

CHAPTER 7

1. Tillich, *Dynamics of Faith*, 1–4.

2. David H. Kelsey, *The Uses of Scripture in Recent Theology* (Philadelphia: Fortress Press, 1975), 74.

3. Ibid., 77. See Rudolf Bultmann, *Theology of the New Testament*, trans. Kendrick Grobel, vol. 2 (New York: Charles Scribner's Sons, 1955), 237–41.

4. E. M. Forster, *Maurice: A Novel* (New York: W. W. Norton, 1971;

paperback, 1981); Hermann Hesse, *Siddhartha*, trans. Hilda Rosner (New York: New Directions, 1951); Toni Morrison, *Sula* (New York: Alfred A. Knopf, 1973; New American Library, Plume, 1982); Lorde, *Sister Outsider*; and Beth Brant, *Mohawk Trail* (Ithaca, N.Y.: Firebrand, 1985).
  5. Hesse, *Siddhartha*, 85.
  6. Morrison, *Sula*, 118.
  7. Lorde, *Sister Outsider*, 115, 123, and "There Is No Hierarchy of Oppressions," 9.
  8. Brant, *Mohawk Trail*, 46–47.
  9. See Noel Greig, "Introduction," in *Edward Carpenter, Selected Writings*, vol. 1, *Sex* (London: GMP, 1984); Hubert Kennedy, *Ulrichs: The Life and Works of Karl Heinrich Ulrichs, Pioneer of the Modern Gay Movement* (Boston: Alyson, 1988); Phyllis Grosskurth, ed., *The Memoirs of John Addington Symonds* (New York: Random House, 1984); Williams, *The Spirit and the Flesh*, 32, 58, 62–63, 73, 83, 194, 244–46, 290 n. 37; Will Roscoe, "Strange Country This: Images of Berdaches and Warrior Women," in *Gay American Indians*, comp., and Will Roscoe, ed., *Living the Spirit: A Gay American Indian Anthology* (New York: St. Martin's, 1988), 67–69; William Moritz, "Seven Glimpses of Walt Whitman," in Mark Thompson, ed., *Gay Spirit: Myth and Meaning* (New York: St. Martin's, 1987), 131–51; Gloria T. Hull, "'Under The Days': The Buried Life and Poetry of Angelina Weld Grimke," in Barbara Smith, ed., *Home Girls: A Black Feminist Anthology* (New York: Kitchen Table/Women of Color Press, 1983), 73–82; Frank Rector, *The Nazi Extermination of Homosexuals* (New York: Stein and Day, 1981), 25, 103–5, 154, 161; Jonathan Katz, "1914: Dr. Magnus Hirschfeld," in *Gay American History*, 151–53; Gertrude Stein, *Everybody's Autobiography* (New York: Random House, 1937; Vintage, 1973); Gertrude Stein, "The Autobiography of Alice B. Toklas," in Carl Van Vechten, *Selected Writings of Gertrude Stein* (New York: Random House, 1962; Vintage, 1972), 1–237; Linda Simon, *The Biography of Alice B. Toklas* (Garden City, N.Y.: Doubleday, 1977); Richard Ellmann, *Oscar Wilde* (New York: Alfred A. Knopf, 1988); Richard Ormrod, *Una Troubridge: The Friend of Radclyffe Hall* (New York: Caroll & Graf, 1985); Lorraine Bethel, "'This Infinity of Conscious Pain': Zora Neale Hurston and the Black Female Tradition," and Gloria T. Hull, "Researching Alice Dunbar-Nelson: A Personal and Literary Perspective," in Gloria T. Hull, Patricia Bell Scott, and Barbara Smith, eds., *All the Women Are White, All the Blacks Are Men, But Some of Us Are Brave* (Old Westbury, N.Y.: Feminist Press, 1982), 176–95; Essex Hemphill, "Looking for Langston: An Interview with Isaac Julien," and Joseph Beam, "James Baldwin: Not a Bad Legacy, Brother," in Essex Hemphill, ed., *Brother to Brother: New Writings by Black Gay Men* (Boston: Alyson, 1991), 174–80, 184–86; and Dorothy J. Farnan, *Auden in Love* (New York: Simon & Schuster, 1984).

For many other less well-known contributors to lesbian/gay/bisexual tradition, see Katz, *Gay American History*.

10.   See Alice Walker, "A Name Is Sometimes an Ancestor Saying Hi, I'm with You," in *Living by the Word: Selected Writings, 1973–1987* (San Diego: Harcourt Brace Jovanovich, 1988), 97–98.

11.   Lorde, *Sister Outsider*, 56.

12.   See Nelson, *Embodiment*, 19–36, 236–71; and Harrison, *Making the Connections*, 135–36, and *Our Right To Choose*, 135–36.

13.   Harrison, *Making the Connections*, 135–36.

14.   Lorde, *Sister Outsider*, 53, 57.

15.   Ibid., 53, 57, 58.

16.   Ibid., 58.

17.   Dag Hammarskjold, *Markings*, trans. Leif Sjoberg and W. H. Auden (Sweden: Albert Bonniers Forlag, 1963; New York: Alfred A. Knopf, 1964; Ballantine, 1983), 43.

18.   Audre Lorde, *A Burst of Light* (Ithaca, N.Y.: Firebrand, 1988), 130.

19.   Forster, "Terminal Note," in *Maurice*, 250.

20.   Merchant/Ivory, producers, *Maurice*, Cinecom Entertainment Group and Film Four International (Irvine, Calif.: Lorimar Home Video, 1987).

21.   Forster, *Maurice*, 13–15.

22.   Forster, "Terminal Note," in *Maurice*, 250.

23.   Ibid., 250–51.

24.   See Greig, "Introduction," in *Edward Carpenter*, 55, 58. Greig's biographical piece, 9–77, is my primary source for information about Carpenter.

25.   Greig, *Edward Carpenter*, 58–66. See also Katz, *Gay American History*, 152, 320–21, 357–58, 379, 393; and Katz, *Gay/Lesbian Almanac*, 160, 250–54, 296–97, 308–9, 336–37, 354, 367–70, 395–97, 414, 430.

26.   See Greig, *Edward Carpenter*, 54–60.

27.   Forster, "Terminal Note," in *Maurice*, 249.

28.   Ibid., 249–50, 252.

29.   Greig, *Edward Carpenter*, 9, 293 n. 2.

30.   Licata, "The Homosexual Rights Movement in the United States," 178.

31.   For accounts of the Stonewall rebellion, see D'Emilio, *Sexual Politics, Sexual Commodities*, 231–33, 246–47; Shilts, *The Mayor of Castro Street*, 41–42; Marotta, *The Politics of Homosexuality*, 71–76; Robert Amsel, "Back to Our Future?: A Walk on the Wild Side of Stonewall," *Advocate* (Los Angeles), 15 September 1987, 36–39, 44–49; Lucian Truscott IV, "Gay

Power Comes to Sheridan Square," *Village Voice* (New York), 3 July 1969, 18; Rechy, *The Sexual Outlaw—A Documentary*, 186–89.

32.   *The New Oxford Annotated Bible*, 87.

33.   Sedgwick, *Epistemology of the Closet*, 67–68.

34.   Forster, *Maurice*; and Merchant/Ivory, *Maurice*.

35.   Greig, *Edward Carpenter*, 15.

36.   King, *Why We Can't Wait*, 34.

CHAPTER 8

1.   Snyder, *Turtle Island*, 106, 108.

2.   See *Encyclopedia of Religion*, s.v. "Covenant," by Delbert R. Hillers; *Interpreter's Dictionary of the Bible*, s.v. "Covenant," by G. E. Mendenhall; *Encyclopedia of Christianity*, s.v. "Covenants, Biblical," by Harry Buis; and *Encyclopaedia of Religion and Ethics*, s.v. "Covenant," by John Herkless.

3.   1 Samuel 20:42.

4.   Song of Songs 2:16; 6:3.

5.   See Trible, *God and the Rhetoric of Sexuality*, 144–65.

6.   Matthew 22:34–40; Mark 12:28–34; and Luke 10:25–28.

7.   Heyward, *Our Passion for Justice*, 53. See also Carter Heyward, *The Redemption of God: A Theology of Mutual Relation* (Washington, D.C.: University Press of America, 1982), and *Touching Our Strength*.

8.   Exodus 1:1–14; Amos 5:21–24; Micah 6:6–8; and John 4:1–42.

9.   See Genesis 16:1–16; 21:9–21; 2 Samuel 13:1–22; Judges 11:29–40; 19:1–30 (also, commentary by Trible, *Texts of Terror*); Colossians 3:18–4:1; 1 Peter 2:18–3:7; and Ephesians 5:21–6:9.

10.   Amos 5:24; Mic. 6:8; Matt. 22:34–40, 25:31–46; Mark 12:28–34; Luke 4:18, 10:25–28.

11.   Lorde, *A Burst of Light*, 130.

12.   Hammarskjold, *Markings*, 12, 43.

13.   Romans 12:6a.

14.   Lorde, *A Burst of Light*, 130.

15.   Luke 7:1–10; 18:9–14; John 3:1–15; 4:46–54; and Matthew 8:5–13.

16.   Mark 14:3–9; Matthew 26:6–13; and John 12:1–8. *The New Oxford Annotated Bible*, 1234.

17.   Cherrie Moraga, "The Welder," in *This Bridge Called My Back: Writings by Radical Women of Color*, ed. Cherrie Moraga and Gloria Anzaldua (New York: Kitchen Table/Women of Color Press, 1981), 219–20.

18.   Ibid.

19. Ibid.
20. Ibid.
21. Ibid.
22. For a discussion of "conflict as . . . a feature of virtually every Indian woman writer," see Paula Gunn Allen, *The Sacred Hoop: Recovering the Feminine in American Indian Traditions* (Boston: Beacon Press, 1986), 165–83.
23. Matthew 10:34–36 and Luke 12:49–53.
24. Mark 16:8.
25. *The New Oxford Annotated Bible*, 1391–92.
26. Snyder, *Turtle Island*, 108–9, and John [Fire] Lame Deer and Richard Erdoes, *Lame Deer: Seeker of Visions* (New York: Simon & Schuster, 1972; Washington Square, Pocket, 1976), 108–28. See also Allen, *The Sacred Hoop*, 54–75.

Selected Bibliography

Boswell, John. *Christianity, Social Tolerance, and Homosexuality: Gay People in Western Europe from the Beginning of the Christian Era to the Fourteenth Century.* Chicago: University of Chicago Press, 1980.

Brant, Beth. *Mohawk Trail.* Ithaca, N.Y.: Firebrand, 1985.

Brooten, Bernadette J. "Paul's View on the Nature of Women and Female Homoeroticism." In *Immaculate and Powerful: The Female in Sacred Image and Social Reality,* edited by Clarissa W. Atkinson, Constance H. Buchanan, and Margaret R. Miles, 61–87. Boston: Beacon Press, 1985.

Brown, Peter. *The Body and Society: Men, Women, and Sexual Renunciation in Early Christianity.* New York: Columbia University Press, 1988.

Brueggemann, Walter. "The Convenanted Family: A Zone for Humanness." *Journal of Current Social Issues* 14 (1977): 18–23.

Bultmann, Rudolf. *Theology of the New Testament.* Vol. 2. Translated by Kendrick Grobel. New York: Charles Scribner's Sons, 1955.

Cady, Joseph. "'Drum-Taps' and Nineteenth-Century Male Homosexual Literature." In *Walt Whitman: Here and Now,* edited by J. P. Kreig, 49–59. Westport, Conn.: Greenwood, 1985.

Driver, S. R. "The Book of Leviticus." *The Sacred Books of the Old and New Testaments.* New York: Dodd, Mead, 1898.

————. *Notes on the Hebrew Text and the Topography of the Books of Samuel with an Introduction in Hebrew Palaeography and the Ancient Versions.* Oxford: Clarendon, 1913.

Falk, Marcia. *The Song of Songs: A New Translation and Interpretation.* San Francisco: Harper, 1990.

Forster, E. M. *Maurice: A Novel.* New York: W. W. Norton, 1971, 1981.

Foucault, Michel. *The History of Sexuality.* Vol. 1, *An Introduction.* Translated by Robert Hurley. Paris: Editions Gallimard, 1976; New York: Pantheon, 1978; Vintage, 1980.

Freire, Paulo. *Pedagogy of the Oppressed,* translated by Myra Bergman Ramos. New York: Continuum, 1985.

Fromm, Erich. *You Shall Be As Gods: A Radical Interpretation of the Old Testament and Its Tradition.* New York: Holt, Rinehart & Winston, 1966; Henry Holt, Owl, 1991.

Gottwald, Norman K. *The Hebrew Bible: A Socio-Literary Introduction.* Philadelphia: Fortress Press, 1985.

————. *The Tribes of Yahweh: A Sociology of the Religion of Liberated Israel, 1250–1050 B.C.E.* Maryknoll, N.Y.: Orbis, 1979.

Greig, Noel, ed. *Edward Carpenter, Selected Writings.* Vol. 1, *Sex.* London: GMP, 1984.

Hammarskjold, Dag. *Markings,* translated by Leif Sjoberg and W. H. Auden. Sweden: Albert Bonniers Forlag, 1963; New York: Alfred A. Knopf, 1964; Ballantine, 1983.

Harrison, Beverly Wildung. *Making the Connections: Essays in Feminist Christian Social Ethics,* edited by Carol Rubb. Boston: Beacon Press, 1985.

————. *Our Right to Choose: Toward a New Ethic of Abortion.* Boston: Beacon Press, 1983.

Hasbany, Richard, ed. *Homosexuality and Religion.* New York: Haworth, 1989.

Hesse, Hermann. *Siddhartha,* translated by Hilda Rosner. New York: New Directions, 1951.

Heyward, Carter. *Our Passion for Justice: Images of Power, Sexuality, and Liberation.* New York: The Pilgrim Press, 1984.

————. *The Redemption of God: A Theology of Mutual Relation.* Washington, D.C.: University Press of America, 1982.

————. *Touching Our Strength: The Erotic as Power and the Love of God.* San Francisco: Harper & Row, 1989.

Hunt, Scott A. "An Unspoken Tragedy: Suicide Among Gay and Lesbian Youth." *Christopher Street,* 14 (1992): 28–30.

Jackson, George. *Soledad Brother: The Prison Letters of George Jackson.* New York: Bantam, 1970.

Kelsey, David H. *The Uses of Scripture in Recent Theology.* Philadelphia: Fortress Press, 1975.

King, Martin Luther, Jr. *Why We Can't Wait.* New York: New American Library, Mentor, 1964.

Lame Deer, John (Fire), and Richard Erdoes. *Lame Deer: Seeker of Visions.* New York: Simon & Schuster, 1972; Washington Square, Pocket, 1976.

Lerner, Gerda. *The Creation of Patriarchy.* New York: Oxford University Press, 1986.

Lorde, Audre. *A Burst of Light.* Ithaca, N.Y.: Firebrand, 1988.

———. *Sister Outsider: Essays and Speeches.* Trumansburg, N.Y.: Crossing, 1984.

———. "There Is No Hierarchy of Oppressions." *Interracial Books for Children Bulletin* 14, nos. 3, 4 (1983): 9.

Moraga, Cherrie, and Gloria Anzaldua, eds. *This Bridge Called My Back: Writings by Radical Women of Color.* New York: Kitchen Table/ Women of Color, 1981.

Nelson, James B. *Embodiment: An Approach to Sexuality and Christian Theology.* Minneapolis: Augsburg, 1978.

Niebuhr, Reinhold. *Leaves from the Notebook of a Tamed Cynic.* Chicago: Willett, Clark and Colby, 1929.

North, Robert. *Sociology of the Biblical Jubilee.* Analecta Biblica Investigationes Scientificae in Res Biblicas 4. Rome: Pontifical Biblical Institute, 1954.

Noth, Martin. *A History of Pentateuchal Traditions,* translated by Bernhard W. Anderson. Englewood Cliffs, N.J.: Prentice Hall, 1972.

———. *Leviticus: A Commentary,* translated by J. E. Anderson. Old Testament Library. Philadelphia: Westminster, 1965.

Nouwen, Henri J. M. *Creative Ministry.* Garden City, N.Y.: Image Books, 1979.

Rosenfeld, Mordecai. "Sodom and the Constitution." *New York Law Journal,* 7 October 1986:2.

Sedgwick, Eve Kosofsky. *Epistemology of the Closet.* Berkeley and Los Angeles: University of California Press, 1990.

Snyder, Gary. *Turtle Island.* New York: New Directions, 1974.

Tillich, Paul. *Dynamics of Faith.* New York: Harper & Brothers, 1957; Harper Torchbook, 1958.

Trible, Phyllis. *God and the Rhetoric of Sexuality.* Overtures to Biblical Theology Series. Philadelphia: Fortress Press, 1978.

———. *Texts of Terror: Literary-Feminist Readings of Biblical Narratives.* Overtures to Biblical Theology Series. Philadelphia: Fortress Press, 1984.

Truscott, Lucian, IV. "Gay Power Comes to Sheridan Square." *Village Voice* (New York), 3 July 1969, 18.

Wiesel, Elie. *A Jew Today*, translated by Marion Wiesel. New York: Random House, 1978; Vintage, 1979.

Williams, Walter L. *The Spirit and the Flesh: Sexual Diversity in American Indian Culture*. Boston: Beacon Press, 1986.

Index